Exploring Practitioner Research in Further Education

Exploring Practitioner Research in Further Education unpacks how people in the Further Education (FE) sector undertake research and the impact it has had on the world around them.

Using a newly developed writing framework and offering a practitioner view of approaching and conducting work in the FE system, this book demystifies the process of undertaking research by showcasing the readers' peers at various stages of the research journey. It draws together research work from general and specialist FE colleges, adult and community learning, offender learning, work-based training, and college-based higher education across the UK. Within these contexts, it makes links to theoretical and practical arguments regarding the usefulness of practitioner-led research. Uniquely, the chapters also explore practitioner- or sector-led models for developing practitioner research within a classroom, within an organisation, and across multiple organisations.

Including a range of diverse voices to represent the breadth of FE, this book provides a framework for research, in addition to a space for each author's authentic voice. This will be a useful text for all teacher educators, professional development leads, senior leaders, and practising teachers and lecturers across the FE sector.

Kerry Scattergood is Lecturer in Adult Literacy at Solihull College & University Centre, UK.

Samantha Jones is Principal Lecturer at the University of Hertfordshire, UK.

'This book is a vital resource for anyone involved in post-compulsory education, from practitioners seeking to improve their craft to leaders looking to foster a culture of research within their institutions. Each chapter is a timely and valuable contribution: empowering practitioners to become researchers, fostering a culture of continuous improvement and innovation within the FE sector.'

Amy Woodrow, *Director of Student Experience, Quality and Safeguarding, City of Bristol College, UK*

'As a Further Education based research practitioner and research lead, the need to grow the practitioner research within the sector cannot be clearer to me. This book contains a plethora of examples about how this has been done and provides a range of examples that can elucidate the process and motivate readers to start to carry out similar research themselves. It is also a book which demonstrates to the powers that be (like the Department for Education and OFSTED) that there is a growing, and thriving, research community in the Post-16 sector which they ignore at their peril.'

Debi Saunders *(She/Her), Senior Quality and Compliance Officer, York College, UK*

'Research should be "rooted in…curiosity" and "made public", asserted Lawrence Stenhouse, a great champion of practitioner researcher. Edited by Sam Jones and Kerry Scattergood, this book is fine example of this as it showcases 12 further education-based practitioner research stories and "maps" FE's research organisations. As such, it will be of great interest to academics researching the sector and an essential and valuable resource to those working in the sector who want to do some practitioner research. Here are three reasons why. First, it provides excellent examples of how to do and write up practitioner research that will inspire aspiring researchers in the sector to "take action". Second, it offers lesson learned from doing practitioner research so that aspiring researchers can build on them rather than trying to find the same "trail of breadcrumbs" as the editors when they started out. Third, these stories reflect the diversity of this most diverse of sectors, showing the aspiring researcher that practitioner research can be done in their setting too. So, if you are curious about the value of practitioner research to an individual or organisation, how to do it or how to write it up, this book is a great place to start.'

Dr David Powell, *University of Huddersfield, UK*

Exploring Practitioner Research in Further Education

Sharing Good Practice

Edited by Kerry Scattergood and Samantha Jones

LONDON AND NEW YORK

Designed cover image: © Getty Images

First published 2025
by Routledge
4 Park Square, Milton Park, Abingdon, Oxon OX14 4RN

and by Routledge
605 Third Avenue, New York, NY 10158

Routledge is an imprint of the Taylor & Francis Group, an informa business

© 2025 selection and editorial matter, Kerry Scattergood and Samantha Jones; individual chapters, the contributors

The right of Kerry Scattergood and Samantha Jones to be identified as the authors of the editorial material, and of the authors for their individual chapters, has been asserted in accordance with sections 77 and 78 of the Copyright, Designs and Patents Act 1988.

All rights reserved. No part of this book may be reprinted or reproduced or utilised in any form or by any electronic, mechanical, or other means, now known or hereafter invented, including photocopying and recording, or in any information storage or retrieval system, without permission in writing from the publishers.

Trademark notice: Product or corporate names may be trademarks or registered trademarks, and are used only for identification and explanation without intent to infringe.

British Library Cataloguing-in-Publication Data
A catalogue record for this book is available from the British Library

Library of Congress Cataloging-in-Publication Data
Names: Scattergood, Kerry, 1977- editor. | Jones, Samantha, 1973- editor.
Title: Exploring practitioner research in further education : sharing good practice / Edited by Kerry Scattergood and Samantha Jones.
Description: Abingdon, Oxon ; New York, NY : Routledge, 2025. | Includes bibliographical references and index. | Summary: "Exploring Practitioner Research in Further Education unpacks how people in the FE sector undertake research and the impact it has had on the world around them. Using a newly developed writing framework and offering a practitioner view of approaching and conducting work in the Further Education (FE) system, this book demystifies the process of undertaking research by showcasing the readers' peers at various stages of the research journey. It draws together research work from general and specialist FE colleges, adult and community learning, offender learning, work-based training, and college-based higher education across the UK. Within these contexts it makes links to theoretical and practical arguments regarding the usefulness of practitioner-led research. Uniquely, chapters also explore practitioner or sector-led models for developing practitioner research within a classroom, within an organisation and across multiple organisations. Including a range of diverse voices to represent the breadth of FE, this book provides a framework for research, in addition to a space for each author's authentic voice. This will be a useful text for all teacher educators, professional development leads, senior leaders and practising teachers and lecturers across the FE sector"-- Provided by publisher.
Identifiers: LCCN 2024040786 (print) | LCCN 2024040787 (ebook) | ISBN 9781032826158 (hardback) | ISBN 9781032824734 (paperback) | ISBN 9781003505389 (ebook)
Subjects: LCSH: Continuing education--Research--Great Britain. | Education, Higher--Research--Great Britain.
Classification: LCC LC5256.G7 E97 2025 (print) | LCC LC5256.G7 (ebook) | DDC 378.125--dc23/eng/20241107
LC record available at https://lccn.loc.gov/2024040786
LC ebook record available at https://lccn.loc.gov/2024040787

ISBN: 978-1-032-82615-8 (hbk)
ISBN: 978-1-032-82473-4 (pbk)
ISBN: 978-1-003-50538-9 (ebk)

DOI: 10.4324/9781003505389

Typeset in Galliard
by KnowledgeWorks Global Ltd.

Dedicated to our girls: Rose, Olivia, Lily, and Rosie.

Contents

List of contributors — *xii*
Foreword — *xv*
Preface — *xix*
Acknowledgements — *xxi*
Glossary — *xxii*

Introduction — 1

Mapping the sector: Further Education research organisations — 8
SAM JONES

PART I
Developing pedagogy — 19

1 Changing the lens: Developing teaching practice through taking a diffractive and dialogical approach to self and peer observation — 21
FRANCINE WARREN

2 Shaping practice and pedagogy in offender learning — 31
KERRY SCATTERGOOD

3 Teach the Teacher: Tackling a failure mindset with GCSE resit learners in Further Education through a 'bridging the empathy gap' intervention — 38
RACHEL ARNOLD

4   Investigating the teaching of agriculture in Further
    Education in England   49
    CATHERINE LLOYD

PART II
Overcoming barriers in the sector   57

5   Reducing barriers to learning opportunities for
    healthcare professionals to improve attendance   59
    KATIE BARRETT

6   Time: The hidden challenge for course leaders for
    college-based higher education   67
    CLARE SUTTON

7   Making learning diaries meaningful for learners in the
    community   77
    CHLOË HYNES

PART III
Models for practitioner research in FE   89

8   Coleg Sir Gar Coleg Ceredigion: The evolution of our
    Culture of Curiosity   91
    BRYONY EVETT HACKFORT

9   The progress of research and scholarship in Scottish
    colleges: Charting some key developments   102
    PATRICK O'DONNELL AND CHRISTINE CALDER

10 The power of community: Developing intergenerational
    learning spaces   111
    FEY COLE

11 Developing the capacity for, and use of, practitioner
    research: The Research College Group   118
    SAMANTHA JONES

PART IV
Stories of leadership 127

12 Unblocking the FE leadership pipeline: Understanding
today's senior leaders in order to inspire tomorrow's 129
DR REBECCA GATER

Conclusion 141
SAM JONES AND KERRY SCATTERGOOD

Index *148*

List of contributors

Rachel Arnold
Rachel is an English Lecturer and Teaching & Learning Coach at Solihull College & University Centre with nine years of FE experience. She holds a Master's degree in Educational Leadership & Improvement and is pursuing a PhD in Education at the University of Cambridge.
   LinkedIn: https://linkedin.com/in/rachel-arnold-395273221

Katie Barrett
Katie manages specialist counselling and support services within the NHS and has previous experience managing and co-ordinating child and adult bereavement, specialist palliative care and cancer support services. In 2023, she gained a post-graduate certificate in education (PGCE) to support her role in providing training and education to Health Care Professionals.

Christine Calder
Christine Calder has worked in Further Education for over 20 years teaching sport and fitness before moving to Academic Development department. Her remit covers teaching qualifications for college lecturers as well as professional learning, and she has interests in all things pedagogical, particularly education for sustainable development.
   @CVCalder

Fey Cole
Fey is a Curriculum Manager in a Further/Higher Education College in Northern Ireland. Fey has been a Lecturer of Early Childhood Education for many years and is the author of *An Educator's Guide to PBL* and *Intergenerational Practice in Schools and Settings*.
   Linktr.ee: https://linktr.ee/Fey_Cole

Rebecca Gater
Rebecca is the Principal and Chief Executive of Solihull College & University Centre. She is a passionate ambassador for FE and has worked in colleges for 25 years. Rebecca was awarded a Doctorate in Education in 2021

for her research on FE senior leadership. Her most recent publications include a chapter in the 2023 book *Pastoral Care in Education: New Directions for New Times* and an International Women's Day article 'Flipping women: re-narrativising women in FE leadership.'
LinkedIn: www.linkedin.com/in/dr-rebecca-gater-69969b79
X: @GaterRebecca

Bryony Evett Hackfort
Bryony is the Director of Teaching, Learning and Education for Coleg Sir Gar and Coleg Ceredigion. Bryony made the move into the leadership of teaching and learning in 2018 and has made the most of every opportunity to establish links, networks, and projects driven to champion the FE sector.
LinkedIn: https://linkedin.com/in/bryony-evett-hackfort-5b4808257?

Chloë Hynes
Chloë is an experienced ESOL and English practitioner who has taught in many areas of FE including ACL, private language schools, colleges, and ITPs. She is a teacher trainer and a mentor with a passion for digital literacies and the value of action research.
www.linkedin.com/in/chloehynes
X: @ChloeFibonacci

Samantha Jones
Sam is a Principal Lecturer at the University of Hertfordshire. Sam previously worked in FE where she was instrumental in the development of practitioner researcher communities, notably #FEResearchmeet and the Research College Group, winning the TES FE Teacher of the Year in 2019 in recognition of this work. Her research work currently focuses on practitioner research. A strong proponent for practitioners owning and articulating their knowledge, in 2022 she edited *Great FE Teaching: Sharing Good Practice*.
https://www.linkedin.com/in/sam-jones-uk/
https://www.researchgate.net/profile/Samantha-Jones-39

Catherine Lloyd
Catherine has worked in Further Education for over 25 years. She undertook an EdD with the Institute of Education UCL which she completed in 2018. Her research interests include leadership and management, and vocational pedagogy within the FE sector.

Patrick O'Donnell
Patrick O'Donnell has worked at Perth UHI – an academic partner of the University of the Highlands and Islands – for more than two decades teaching STEM. Patrick has worked closely with colleagues from other Scottish universities, and his most recent collaborative works include the evolution of university libraries as learning spaces: DOI: https://doi.org/10.1080/13614533.2021.1906718.

Kerry Scattergood

Kerry is a lecturer in adult literacy at Solihull College & University Centre and has been teaching in further and adult education for over 20 years. She is also FE Research Lead within her college, with a passion for raising the capacity for practitioner research within the FE sector. She involved in the #FEResearchMeet movement, is West Midlands convener for the LSRN, a committee member of the ARPCE, and is a founding member of the Research College Group.

LinkedIn: https://linkedin.com/in/kerry-scattergood

ResearchGate: (7) Kerry Scattergood (researchgate.net)

X: @KMScattergood

Clare Sutton

Clare is a Senior Lecturer in Education at Teesside University. Her role includes course leading the PGCE in Primary (QTS), and she is a link tutor for education-based courses with the college partnership. Clare is a PhD researcher at Durham University, focusing on course leaders for college-based higher education.

LinkedIn: linkedin.com/in/clare-sutton-fhea-bb224615b/

X: @ClareSu26617344

Francine Warren

Francine is an Advanced Practitioner (HE) at the LTE Group, supporting lecturers at UCEN Manchester. She has taught in further and higher education. With a background in Post Compulsory Education Training (PCET) and Teacher Education, her interests include the scholarship of teaching and learning (SoTL) and practitioner research. Francine is a committee member of the ARPCE.

LinkedIn: https://www.linkedin.com/in/francine-warren-474015153?

Foreword

I am deeply grateful to Kerry and Samantha for inviting me to write a foreword to this excellent book. Most of my research career over the last half-century has been spent supporting and undertaking educational research in and on Further Education. For the last 30 years, I have been privileged to be Editor-in Chief of the Taylor & Francis international peer-reviewed journal, *Research in Post-Compulsory Education* (*RPCE*). That publication, established by Triangle Journals, a small independent UK publishing company, was the first journal in the world to cover the broad spectrum of post-compulsory education. From the outset, *RPCE*'s particular focus was practitioner research, commissioning and encouraging contributions from teachers and researchers throughout the PCE sector, including, but not restricted to, Further Education, community and adult education, and college-based higher education. The journal was not initially associated with any one institution or learned society, but through my own close connection with the Association for Research in Post-Compulsory Education (ARPCE) (formerly the Further Education Research Association, FERA), the Editorial Board of the journal became synonymous with the Organising Committee of ARPCE. This has been a most productive relationship, for example, with the journal publishing special issues featuring the best of the presentations at the association's international conferences, held biennially at Harris Manchester College, Oxford. To this day, *RPCE* continues to encourage and publish original research on Further Education and beyond. As Editor, I can report that *RPCE* is flourishing and receives many more potential contributions that it can possibly accommodate. Increasingly, these have been sourced internationally, demonstrating the growing interest in research on the PCE sector worldwide. To what can we attribute this growing interest in research in post-compulsory education?

Back in 1996, I was able to have published in the UK's leading generic education research publication, *British Educational Research Journal*, an article titled 'Why is Research Invisible in Further Education?' (Elliott 1996).

This was based upon my own research as a lecturer in Further Education undertaking a part-time Doctor of Education degree at the University of Bristol. My tutors encouraged me in pursuit of answers to my questions about research and Further Education, recognising, as I found through my own experience and practice, that research did seem to be invisible throughout the sector. Certainly in terms of published academic research, there was a dearth of studies featuring FE, whilst early years, schools and higher education seemed to be very well represented.

Historically, the sector has been significantly underrepresented as a focus of educational research. Peters (1967), in his survey of the sector, found that there was a preponderance of small-scale and scattered research, largely undertaken by individuals pursuing higher degrees, with a consequent lack of feedback into practice and policy of such results as were obtained. He also noted a lack of established links between FE colleges and university institutes and departments of education, and an overall poor liaison between, 'on the one hand, practitioners and policy makers who know the problems but lack time or training to conduct research, and on the other, research workers who may not be fully in touch with the problems' (1967, pp. 271–272).

It is certainly instructive to track the progress of FE research over the last period. In my 1996 BERJ article, I made an argument for the centrality of a supportive research culture to facilitating or fostering research in FE, and I identified a number of barriers to a research culture in FE. These included:

- Few staff working in FE with higher degrees or research experience,
- Underfunding of staff training and development,
- Incorporation squeezing college budgets,
- Inflexible staff contracts and organisation structures,
- High staff workloads,
- Absence of research posts in FE,
- Discouragement of 'academic drift' by managers and policy-makers,
- Research and evaluation predominantly external functions,
- Lack of FE/HE research links and partnerships,
- Teaching, not research, is the core activity,
- Any available research funding focuses on QA,
- Limited library facilities,
- Cross-subsidy of research disallowed or not encouraged,
- FE climate prioritises problem solving, coping, and quick answers,
- FE-located work underrepresented in the literature of educational research,
- The competitive FE culture discourages collaborative research activity,
- Narrow conceptions of research in FE.

This is quite a list, and readers might find themselves wondering what has changed....

Roughly a decade ago I was prompted to collaborate with my good friend and colleague Dr Carla Solvason in a piece of work examining similar themes in college-based higher education (Solvason and Elliott, 2013). This new study drew upon a small sample of lecturers who belong to a Further and Higher Education Early Years Partnership. Through the participants' voices and perspectives, we identified continuing dissonance and issues of research marginalisation, and also highlighted contemporary educational discourse, with its predominant focus upon measurable value at the expense of values, as a key factor in sustaining a culture that is antithetic to thoughtful reflection and research. We identified the development of a 'collaborative centralised' research community as critical to an alternative possibility for future research in Further Education. I was sharply reminded of our propositions along these lines when I came across the introduction of this current book which explores the further potential for practitioner research in FE, and reflects that 'the most successful research cultures are mutual: simultaneously bottom up and top down.'

Doubtless some progress has been made. The growth of college-based higher education through FE/HE partnerships and independently has been encouraging. More FE-based research is being reported and funded, and there is some fine practice reported in the present book. What is more questionable is the degree to which colleges – as opposed to practitioner researchers themselves – are in practice influenced by such research. I suppose this is a question ultimately about leadership in the sector. I have always wondered to what extent leadership programmes promote the active application of research as opposed to using research as a useful repository of leadership models and methods that might be applied in colleges. More deeply, how far are college leaders able to apply that critical questioning stance so essential to practitioner research to their own leadership practice? And here I am thinking not only of the chief executive and their senior management team but of middle managers who set targets and boundaries for their reports, and not least of the tutor and classroom teacher whose professional identity can be reshaped and invigorated through reflective practice, reflection, and reflexivity.

This book paints a broad canvas of practitioner research in Further Education, and rightly so. There is consideration of both college-level and classroom-level interactions that may foster and facilitate or discourage and disempower such work. There is representation of a wide range of post compulsory education settings throughout the four nations of the UK from specialist colleges and offender learning to work-based training and college-based higher education. There is similar diversity in methodological approaches to research, from learning diaries and observation to video recording and discourse analysis. These different settings and approaches serve to underpin and reinforce a key aim of the book – creating the space for practitioner researchers to sit alongside other forms of knowing and researching the FE sector that inform practice. What results is scholarship of the highest level that will make an original and important contribution to the theoretical literature of Further Education. Finally, I hope that by reading this book, researchers, practitioners, and those with leadership responsibilities are encouraged to value research, recognise its contribution to building good practice throughout Further Education, and form sustainable research communities that embrace risk, innovation, and academic generosity.

Dr Geoffrey Elliott
Professor of Post Compulsory Education
University of Worcester

References

Elliott, G. (1996) 'Why is research invisible in further education?', *British Educational Research Journal*, 22(1), pp. 101–111.

Peters, A. (1967) *British further educations: a critical textbook*. Oxford, Pergamon Press.

Solvason, C. and Elliott, G. (2013) 'Why is research still invisible in further education', *Journal of Learning Development in Higher Education*, (6). doi: 10.47408/jldhe.v0i6.206.

Preface

Kerry Scattergood

One of the things I have learnt, in co-editing this book, is that a preface is an opportunity to tell the story of how and why the book came to be. How this book came into being is such an important part of our journey, and it feels too important not to be told.

In a serendipitous moment, the co-editors came together in a moment of recognition for the importance of such a publication at this moment in time. We have often had similar experiences and made the assumption we are thinking along the same lines, but in hindsight there is a reason we came to the same realisation at the same time. It is because, at that moment in time, we were working within the Research College Group (RCG) together to find ways of not only showcasing Further Education (FE) projects but also enabling the learning to ripple out and have repercussions on the sector. We are both very conscious that there is not much point to research if it isn't used. When I completed my first project, outlined in Chapter 2, I was content with the learning it afforded me, and at the time I didn't realise the implications of that learning not being seen by others. As we explore in the conclusion of this book, there can be some serious downstream consequences of the invisibility of professional learning through research, the worst consequence being losing people from the sector, people who feel under-utilised – or worse – under-valued.

Having identified the importance of a book like this in our times, I turned to the past to see if it is possible to follow the trail of breadcrumbs to where we are now (and also, as all good scholars do, to check this work wasn't already published and somehow we had missed it!). The last volume of this kind, an edited book of Further Education practitioner research projects, was last published in 2005, called *Readings in Post-compulsory Education*. It was no surprise to us that this was a publication born out of the Learning and Skills Research Network (LSRN), as the LSRN has been the one constant showcasing practitioner research for almost 30 years and has very much been the beginnings of our journeys into the wider culture of FE research.

Like Elliott's 1996 infamous paper 'Why is Research Invisible in Further Education?', this volume is full of the importance of, but also the barriers too, good research cultures and practices for FE. We feel, having worked as educators, mentors, and leaders of research alongside practitioners, that some of the lessons we have learnt are too important to remain invisible.

We seek to save future initiatives from having to follow the same trail of breadcrumbs, or even to try to lay new tracks, by sharing and benefiting all from what is known, and to work to protect it from being forgotten in the future. We have learnt from being in and close to professional research that invisibility serves no one well and should not keep this learning in our heads either, any more than our practitioners should. Practice changes practice (Zuber-Skerritt, 2012), and these lessons are what drives us.

This book represents a moment in time, building on the publication of *Great FE Teaching: Sharing Good Practice* (Jones, 2022) and the work from within the RCG to publish practitioners from its member organisations, and we hope all benefit.

References

Elliott, G. (1996) 'Why is research invisible in further education?', *British Educational Research Journal*, 22(1), pp. 101–111. https://doi.org/10.1080/0141192960220107

Hillier, Y. and Thompson, A. (2005) *Readings in post-compulsory education*. London: Continuum.

Jones, S. (2022) *Great FE teaching: sharing good practice*. London: Corwin.

Zuber-Skerritt, O. (2012) *Action research for sustainable development in a turbulent world*. 1st edn. Bingley: Emerald Group Pub. Ltd.

Acknowledgements

We like to thank all the contributors to the book. Without you, there would be no book, and we are eternally grateful for not only your contributions but also the spirit and generosity in which you share your work.

However, like any FE research endeavour, we are very conscious that this work is only possible because of all the incredible people that have come before us and all the people who currently surround us, so we would like to acknowledge the practitioner researchers of the sector, particularly those who are associated with the LSRN, the RCG, the ARPCE, the many college research groups that have sprung up across the sector over the past ten or so years, and of course all those wonderful FEResearchmeet conveners, past, present, and future.

We would like to thank Nigel Hooson for his time and his thinking – both of us have been enriched by our discussions and are great admirers of your work.

Many thanks to Alex Stevenson, at the Learning and Work Institute, for permission to reproduce the RARPA image.

To Debi Saunders of the Research College Group, our gratitude in your generosity and permission to share the RCG data.

A thank you to the editing team at Routledge for all their help and support getting this book from what seemed like an impossible idea to reality. We are grateful for your belief in us.

We would also like to thank our partners for their support and love.

Finally, without getting too gushy, we'd like to celebrate the spirit that pervades the FE sector, the spirit that brought us together and has kept us together, despite one of us who is sadly no longer able to find a home there. It is in the spirit of collegiality and defiance that if we work together, we can make a difference, and, albeit a small one, we like to hope that we have.

Glossary

ACL	Adult and community learning
AoC	Association of Colleges
APs	Academic Partners
ARPCE	Association for Research in Post-Compulsory Education
BCGRN	Bedford College Group Research Network
BERA	British Education Research Association
CAIRN	College Action Inquiry Research Network
CBHE	College-based higher education
CDN	College Development Network
CL	Course leaders
Covid-19	Coronavirus disease caused by the SARS-CoV-2 virus
CPD	Continuous Professional Development
DfBIS	Department for Business, Innovation & Skills (dissolved)
DfE	Department for Education
DfIUS	Department for Innovation, University & Skills (now a part of the DfE)
EMCETT	East Midlands Centre for Excellence in Teacher Training
ETF	Education and Training Foundation
ESOL	English for Speakers of Other Languages
FE	Further Education
FEC	Further Education College
FEDA	Further Education Development Agency (dissolved)
GCSE	General Certificate of Secondary Education
HE	Higher Education
HEFCE	Higher Education Funding Council for England
ILP	Individual Learning Plan
ITE	Initial Teacher Education
LSRN	Learning and Skills Research Network
LWI	Learning and Work Institute
MA	Master's degree in Arts
NCFE	Awarding body, formerly Northern Council for Further Education

NHS	National Health Service
NPM	New Public Management
Ofsted	The Office for Standards in Education, Children's Services and Skills
OLASS	Offenders' Learning and Skills Service
OTL	Observations of teaching and learning
OTLA	Outstanding Teaching, Learning & Assessment projects
PAL	Programme area leaders
PBL	Project-based learning
PCET	Post-compulsory education and training
PCK	Pedagogical content knowledge
PDSA	Plan-do-study-act
PGCE	Post Graduate Certificate in Education
PhD	Doctor of Philosophy
PLAR	Practitioner Led Action Research
PLR	Personal Learning Record
RARPA	Recognising and Recording Progress and Achievement
RCG	Research College Group
R&D	Research and development
SAR	Self Assessment Report
SfL	Skills for Life (a government initiative for delivering adult basic skills)
SMART	Specific, Measurable, Achievable, Realistic, Time-bound targets
SMT	Senior Management Team
TSR	Teacher-student relationships
TTT	Teach the Teacher intervention
UCU	University and College Union
UHI	University and the Highlands and Islands
UHI EO	University and the Highlands and Islands Executive Office
UHI LTA	University and the Highlands and Islands Learning and Teaching Academy
UK	United Kingdom
UNESCO	United Nations Education, Scientific and Cultural Organisation

Introduction

This book is about space, voice, ownership, professionalism, and utility.

It is about space at several levels: it is about creating the space for practitioner researchers to sit alongside side other forms of knowing and researching the Further Education (FE) sector that inform practice; it is about space to experiment with the voices and methods through which we share practice.

The book is about voice: about exploring what researchers from the FE sector can legitimately express about the sector; it is about sharing a variety of voices that express the diversity of the sector, shining a light into those dark corners where others do not travel (to paraphrase Peter Shukie).

It is about ownership: of our voices, of our developing skills as researchers, and of our professionalism and of our practice. It's about owning the space that we work in and the knowledge we use in them and it's about owning our innovations.

It is about professionalism: in researching our practice or the practice of others; it's about our professionalism as teachers and about finding mechanisms to facilitate opportunities to develop our professionalism in ways that suit us.

When we first thought about this book, we wanted a book that made the reader feel 'oh, I could use this in my practice' or 'oh, maybe I could research my own practice'. Although many chapters look at practice, the book has been led by its chapter authors to explore what is interesting to them. More than this, we hope that the simple premise of a curl of excitement and a desire to use or take action upon what is read remains.

This is the utility: to move past researching and disseminating, to researching making change, change to the individuals, change to how we view our knowledge, and change to culture and capacity for research in the sector.

What is the motivation behind the book?

The motivation for creating this book came out of the work we were doing first through two practitioner-led research spaces: FEResearchmeet (Jones et al., 2024) and the Research College Group (RCG) (see Sam Jones' Chapter 11;

also, Chen et al., 2025). The ethos of both, from the beginning, has always been motivated by a need for democratic leadership, by the sector for the sector. From the early days of FEResearchmeet, FE practitioners created the opportunity to share their work with and for themselves, no longer relying on others to create opportunities for them. The RCG picked up this ethos and further developed the possibility of building further capacity from within the sector, not only through developing research skills and leadership but also by exploring different ways of knowing. What we have learnt from these experiences is that the most successful research cultures are mutual: simultaneously bottom up and top down.

The book explores the breadth of practitioner research across the diverse FE sector by drawing together work from general and specialist FE colleges; adult and community learning; offender learning; and work-based training and college-based higher education across England, Northern Ireland, Scotland, and Wales.

The work presented in the book encompasses a broad range of work, from action research focused on improving classroom practice, through to masters, doctoral, and post-doctoral research. These are explored under the section headings of 'developing pedagogy' and 'overcoming barriers in the sector.' It also explores practitioner or sector-led models for developing practitioner research within a classroom, within an organisation, and across multiple organisations.

There are few books aimed at research in FE and even fewer that focus on the narratives and agentic actions of the FE researchers themselves. Commonly, books focused on research tell people 'how to' or discuss results. This book explores how people *have* researched and the impact it has had on the world around them. This is important at a time of increasing interest in FE research. However, it is also important in developing the activity itself.

Creating a writing framework

In developing the idea of the book, the importance of authenticity of voice causes a tension between a need to showcase the work of professionals within the sector and the 'uniform' approach of some research publications. Just like some of the chapter authors explore risk in the work that follows, we as editors were taking a risk by hanging together such different types of research work from across such a diverse sector. It felt extremely important that this authenticity was maintained, yet a clear approach was needed which would incorporate such diversity. After discussing the importance of allowing each chapter author their own opportunity to choose their own language to represent their work, the idea for a framework to bring some unity to the book was developed. The framework used was created by Jones based on the work of Kelchtermans (2021) and Parsons (2021). Furthermore, we recognise this framework is a further opportunity for raising capacity, as is published here for the use of the reader.

The purpose of this specific approach to the framework is to promote parity and unity between the two sites of research and practice. Whereby other approaches may favour the rigor of academic markers, such as BERA's 'close to practice' focusing mainly on literature and methodology as markers of 'good work', this approach enables the good work of practice to be examined through a more relevant lens. This prompts the less experienced researcher to think about some of the markers of good practice-facing work highlighted by Kelchtermans (2021) and Parsons (2021), whilst more experienced researchers can develop their work in ways that meet the academic markers that they have been trained to address. This levels the playing field so everyone can write as equals.

As editors, we were clear to chapter authors that it was their decision where their focus lay, in terms of which of the prompt questions they addressed under each subheading and where they chose to focus their wordcount. The framework is shared below.

Practitioner-led abstract/chapter summary (Jones)

(based on the works of Kelchtermans, 2021 and Parsons, 2021)

1 Research questions and or aims and objectives.
2 Positionality: the position you take in relation to your questions or the object under investigation? How does this reflect your values?
3 Using knowledge: what does existing research say about the object under investigation and which debates or positions are useful to your study?
4 The existing context: what does the existing context, setting, and participants look like, and why does it look like this?
5 Methodology: how have you approached your study (observing or changing practice, selecting participants, collecting data, and ethical considerations)?
6 Findings: What did I find? What changes did I make? How do I see the object of my investigation now? What data do I have that supports these findings? What do I think may be underlying these changes?
7 Conclusions: what are my conclusions and recommendations? Which of these may be specific to my context, and which may be useful to others and why?

Contributions

The 12 chapters that follow are a collection of research stories from across the sector. The first four chapters share projects which develop pedagogy. In the middle section, we have grouped together three chapters which address challenges facing FE professionals. In the third section, we showcase four models for research in FE, one from each of our home nations. In the final section, we explore one piece of research in the under researched area of leadership in FE.

Part 1: Developing pedagogy

In Chapter 1, teacher-educator Francine Warren challenges the idea that teacher observation can simultaneously be performative and developmental and offers a new way of thinking about observations by adopting a diffractive lens and creating a framework, which can be utilised by others for their own purposes. The teachers in the study agreed to video themselves, with the intention of sharing their videos with peers. The aim was to observe each other, not with a view to giving feedback or looking for what 'works', but to talking to each other about what they had seen and ask 'why' and 'what if'. Francine explores the impact on pedagogical awareness through adopting this diffractive lens to enable trainee teachers to have meaningful and developmental, non-judgemental conversations.

Chapter 2 explores a small-scale project in an adult basic skills offender learning setting. Kerry Scattergood explores the development of her practitioner researcher identity through her first steps of researching. She had recognised her learners struggled to advance their writing due to incomplete sentence use and that she wished to explore how tapping into their everyday writing practices might be useful to understanding this. In doing so, she began to explore a wider understanding of the difficulty of moving learning between the domains of college, home, and work. She began to identify the learners' development of identity through their opportunities to write, which became an important aspect of her later work and PhD study.

In Chapter 3, FE GCSE resit teacher Rachel Arnold explores her masters project. The chapter explores an approach to the thorny issue of maths and English GCSE resits. The study addresses a fixed, failure mindset through the 'Teach the Teacher' (TTT) intervention, where students become the experts and teach their teachers a practical skill from their vocational course. This is a really student-focused initiative that reverses the role of student and teacher, to change the relationship between the two, bridging 'the empathy gap'. The findings show positive engagement with the intervention, emphasising the significance of meaningful teacher-student relationships for disengaged learners helps bridge the empathy gap.

Chapter 4 explores agriculture provision and the factors which influence curriculum delivery from a piece of post-doctoral research work. Catherine Lloyd, a Vice-Principal of a land-based college whose role includes line management of those responsible for practical resources, wanted to better understand agriculture provision and the factors which influenced curriculum delivery. Catherine uses a qualitative study to explore the teaching of agriculture to FE students in England, focusing specifically on how teachers identify and address areas of misunderstanding within the subject area when teaching students. Catherine's chapter provides a narrative into her decision-making as she undertakes her project. The chapter begins with an overview of the study before focusing on a specific aspect, following it through from literature review to methodology, findings, and discussion to illustrate the research process and highlight the progressive nature of research as you move from one stage to the next. Catherine provides the background to the study and presents her position in relation to the subject under investigation to give context. The chapter ends by considering the limitations of the study and reflects on issues of quality in research.

Part 2: overcoming barriers in the sector

Katie Barrett, in Chapter 5, outlines an action research project she undertook at her workplace within the NHS whilst completing a PGCE. Katie's chapter is an example of how action research changes not just the researcher's context but also the researcher themselves.

The work explores how reducing barriers to learning opportunities can improve attendance rates at training courses for healthcare professionals. Research was undertaken to identify the barriers faced by healthcare professionals when attending *Bereavement, Grief and Loss* training, and key barriers from data collection and analysis were identified. Katie's findings indicate that management support directly improved attendance, alongside having a positive impact on staff feeling valued. However, she also captures some of the challenges she encountered by the researcher when conducting the study, which are parallel to those faced by healthcare professionals within the NHS context.

In Chapter 6, PhD researcher Clare Sutton investigates issues of time raised by course leaders (CLs) for college-based higher education (CBHE) by asking the questions, how do issues relating to time manifest themselves in the everyday work of CLs? And what are the institutional processes that result in the issues relating to time faced by CLs? Clare takes an institutional ethnographic approach for her research and collects data from interviews with CLs, and members of the management teams in the college as well as through the analysis of texts. Her findings illustrate that the additional work required by CLs for CBHE was not considered when planning their workload and that the issues relating to time stem from a management style inherent in the FE sector where efficiency remains the priority.

Chapter 7 sees Chloë Hynes, a leader in many of the Education and Training Foundation's Action Research programmes, exploring a practitioner action research project which investigates an area of improvement identified in her organisation's Self-Assessment Report (SAR): giving meaningful feedback.

The project was undertaken in an adult and community learning provision and documents Chloë challenging and amending an institutional 'one-size-fits-all' document used to capture learner progress in non-accredited ESOL (English for Speakers of Other Languages) courses.

The project reflects Chloë's values. It is collaborative and involves working alongside the learners to garner support and inspiration in order to develop a 'learner diary'. The diary they co-develop needed to be sufficient in recognising and recording their progress and achievement (RARPA) but also chart their individual learner journeys meaningfully and effectively.

Chloë records how managers were understandably nervous about the challenge to a document they had a responsibility to see implemented; however, when they experienced its effectiveness in practice in the organisation's classrooms, the practitioner research was accepted and the organisation began to approach the documents differently themselves.

Part 3: Models for practitioner research in FE

In Chapter 8, we take a step into Coleg Sir Gar Coleg Ceredigion with their Director of Teaching and Learning and Education. The colleges' vision is to become a centre of excellence for post-compulsory educational research in Wales. Bryony takes us through her development of an inspiring and innovative teaching and learning culture, underpinned by staff research, undertaken by all staff who wish to, regardless of experience. The work aims to inform college practice and empower their staff. The Culture of Curiosity values the importance of supporting our staff to be innovative, creative, brave, and forward thinking in their approach to teaching and learning. Bryony's chapter gives an insight into their journey to create a professional learning culture led by action research, where they started, where they are now, and where they hope to go next with their Culture of Curiosity.

Chapter 9 moves to Scotland where Patrick O'Donnell, an academic partner of the University of the Highlands and Islands, and Christine Calder a leader of an Academic Development department, explore the emergent research and scholarship dynamic within the Scottish FE setting. Their chapter documents two different approaches to the development of research in the sector which has resulted in a modest but nevertheless, steady interest in research and scholarly activities unfolding within Scottish Colleges despite the research not generally be conceptualised as being part of the core character of FE.

In Chapter 10, Fey Cole, a Curriculum Manager in a Further/Higher Education College in Northern Ireland, explores how formal and action research has explored the benefits of the research of intergenerational and project-based learning on student's emotional well-being and educational outcomes. Fey's research investigates the impact these two approaches have on learning outcomes and how it develops a sense of community and belonging within the FE environment. The chapter focuses on how project-based learning can connect students with their local environment and develop the skills required for adopting a sustainable and industry-led focus, and how a creative approach to delivery can build student autonomy in learning and developing positive relationships between students and educators.

In Chapter 11, Samantha (Sam) Jones takes us through a research project undertaken by the RCG, an organisation that convenes post-16 organisations from across to improve the visibility and use of research. Sam's chapter highlights the practices and methodologies developed by the RCG in order to address the constraints and requirements of researching in this sector. Through this lens, Sam argues that contextual and practice-focused work can provide a useful complement to other forms of research, and that the sector has the skills and abilities to lead large research projects itself if barriers are addressed.

Part 4: Stories of leadership in FE

Chapter 12 sees Rebecca Gater, Principal and CEO of Solihull College & University Centre, surveying the professional identities of senior leaders in FE. She investigates the motivations and significant life events that prompted teachers to transition into leadership roles in order to understand how these individuals define their identities, the impact of their life experiences on their career paths, and the critical incidents that influenced their decisions to pursue leadership roles.

Rebecca's chapter has much to tell us about the evolution of leadership in FE, noting a shift from hierarchical, efficiency-driven management to a more inclusive, collaborative approach. It emphasises the importance of authenticity, relationship-building, and strategic accountability in shaping effective leadership. The findings reveal that senior leaders like Rebecca, often perceived as having led privileged lives, are in fact 'ordinary' individuals whose diverse backgrounds and experiences have equipped them with unique leadership qualities. By shedding light on her findings, Rebecca's ultimate goal is to unblock the leadership pipeline and address the impending leadership crisis by rehumanising and revitalising the image of FE leadership.

References

Chen, J., Derrick, J., Duncan, S., Hayward, G., Jones, S. and Smith, L. (2025) 'Doing research or being researched? Debates on 'Close-to-Practice' research from the perspective of the further, adult and vocational education (FAVE) sector', in Wyse, B., Baumfield, V., Mockler, N. and Reardon, M. (eds.) *The BERA-SAGE international handbook of research-informed education policy and practice*. London: SAGE.

Jones, S., Scattergood, K., Rees, J. and Crowther N. (2024) 'FEResearchmeet. A Further Education (FE) practitioner-researcher led initiative to share and develop capacity for research and scholarship across Wales and England: analysing and theorising the period of initial development.' *Research in Post-Compulsory Education*, 29 (3).

Kelchtermans, G. (2021) 'Keeping educational research close to practice', *British Educational Research Journal*, 47(6), pp. 1504–1511.

Parsons, S. (2021) 'The importance of collaboration for knowledge co-construction in 'close-to-practice' research', *British Educational Research Journal*, 47(6), pp. 1490–1499.

Mapping the sector

Further Education research organisations

Sam Jones

In the preface to the book, Kerry discusses following the breadcrumbs to understand what has happened before. She looks back to Hillier and Thompson's (2005) book which has allowed us to map the problems we have faced and the genesis of some of the approaches we have taken to improve visibility of research in the Further Education (FE) sector. This chapter aims to replicate that sense of mapping for this point in time. The map we provide covers the initiatives that have been important to Kerry and I throughout our journey.

The map isn't exhaustive, and nor to did we intend it to be, there are a lot of spaces that are marked 'here be dragons' and as we feel these are for others who have lived in these spaces to map. One of the driving forces for the book and its forerunner 'Great FE Teaching' (Jones, 2022) has been to give individuals the space to express their story in their own words, no third parties narrating or interpreting. This is because we have experienced the empowerment and sense of autonomy that comes with that experience and because we feel the FE sector should speak for itself. As Kerry has said, it is those who practice in FE who are the experts on FE practice, and how could this be otherwise.

So within this chapter, you will find narratives from the recent past, starting with the grandaddy of all FE research movements, the Learning and Skills Research Network (LSRN), we'll move on to a space created in the LSRN, the Bedford College Group Research Network. From here, we'll look at two publication and sharing opportunities, the Association of Research in Post-Compulsory Education and FEResearchmeet, before moving on to the wealth of practitioner research work led by the Education and Training foundation. We will end with the trailblazing Research College Group, the first group of organisations from across the diversity of post-16 provision brought together to research and develop research capacity (Jones, 2018).

Perhaps you will recognise activities you have engaged on and led, giving you a better understanding of not only what went before, but most importantly giving you different views on what could come next.

Learning and Skills Research Network

The role of research in informing practice is becoming more widely understood across education. In the FE and skills sector, this is reflected in the expansion of the Learning and Skills Research Network, the rise of the Research College Group and the creation of the *Research Further* scheme at the Association of Colleges. A new generation of skilled practitioner-researchers is making waves, thanks partly to the Education & Training Foundation's former practitioner research programme at the University of Sunderland[1].

But it wasn't always like this. Back in the 1990s, the profile of research in the sector was lower. Although many colleges were active in development work around curriculum and pedagogy, research was mainly linked to Higher Education (HE) provision in larger colleges[2]. To address this, academic and practitioner researchers were brought together by the Further Education Development Agency (FEDA) in 1996 in a residential workshop on research in FE. Keen to raise the profile of sector research, enthusiasts from this event decided to set up an FE Research Network (FERN, since renamed LSRN). From that day to this, LSRN has championed research and evidence-use in the sector and remains an important element in today's research infrastructure.

The LSRN's enduring role in a turbulent sector is a result of the way it was set up: as an independent and inclusive network rather than an institution, based in the regions and run by activists rather than office-holders. Its original statement of values and purposes still binds it together today[3]. All types of institutions in the sector are welcomed, as well as universities and any relevant public, private or voluntary sector bodies. Volunteers step forward across the regions and nations to organise locally based events and projects.

In the early days, support from FEDA enabled a national conference to be mounted each year with participant numbers eventually reaching 300+. At its peak, leading researchers, principals and ministers addressed the conferences, tackling issues such as widening participation, local economic development and qualification reform. The growing success of these led to funding for regional groups to undertake small-scale collaborative research projects between colleges and universities. They choose locally pertinent topics, such as progression, modern apprenticeship and rural deprivation. An evaluative report *Collaborative Research in Practice*[4] helped tease out factors that held and hindered such collaborations. Activists then developed a set of self-learning units (the *R&D Toolkit*) to enable local groups to develop their skills as researchers and users of evidence[5].

On the abolition of FEDA, core supporters met together in 2006 and decided to continue the LSRN as a voluntary, independent network and called on various bodies to offer support in cash or kind. Twice yearly, workshops were held in London on topical issues in practice and policy, which engaged teachers, leaders, academics and people from a multitude of agencies in research-informed dialogue. Local events took place around the country, wherever a volunteer could muster support. Evidence was debated about issues such as teacher standards, vocational pedagogy and college-based HE, summaries of which were often published in FE Week.

The outbreak of the Covid-19 pandemic in 2020 appeared, at first, to call a halt to the activity of the 23-year-old network. The unexpected upsurge of virtual communications technology in fact opened up a new era. Next-generation activists, at ease with digital technology and social media platforms, started organising sessions online. Paradoxically, participation began to grow as the time and cost of travel were spared. Events proliferated, and soon a Convenors' Group was set up, and a volunteer chair found, to coordinate activity in a light touch way. In effect, coordination of the network had transferred to the next generation, while its non-bureaucratic, collective and voluntary character was retained. Many new people stepped forward to convene groups in new regions, and in Wales and the Crown Dependencies.

With a growing body of active participants, assisted by virtual communications, participants were able to join multiple events and meet people from other regions. A stronger sense of community developed which encouraged the Convenors' Group to organise the first post-pandemic conference. This hugely successful event, in April 2023 at Aston University Conference Centre, created a buzz, as people finally met face-to-face and found common cause. Thanks to a generous offer from the Association of Colleges, a publication was produced based on many of the papers presented.[6]

Looking to the future, a two-year rotation has evolved, to ensure the burden of coordinating the organisation at national level is shared. The LSRN is proving to be a valuable meeting ground for people new to research as well as those involved in higher level research training. The steady stream of volunteers stepping forward to organise activity locally demonstrates once again the resilience of the network in an unsteady sector. Alongside other structures that have sprung up to support research and evidence-use, it looks set to continue playing an important role in developing evidence-informed culture across the sector.

Andrew Morris 13th June 2024

The Bedford College Group Research Network

The Bedford College Group Research Network was not a new idea, but it is a good example of a recent iteration of the model, and one that has been led and developed by researchers from within rather than outside the FE space and is well documented and analysed by Lloyd and Jones (2018).

The network was formed in 2014 with the intention of developing a supportive space for research active members of staff within Bedford College to support each other in researching and developing their identity and skills. Importantly, the network was set up with a view to creating pathways and mechanisms to the feed research work into the senior management team. In this respect, the network shared aims with many others to develop and normalise research in the sector. However, at the time, there were fewer networks that also aimed to ensure that the research work was used to inform the decision-making of the wider college.

In order to achieve this additional aim, the Bedford College Network was required to create, or reinstate, mechanisms into the college to help their work feed into decision-making. This included making work more appealing to our senior team by triangulating several members' research work around Continuous Professional Development (CPD) that had been undertaken in the college to produce a report whose data could be considered not only more robust but was also contextualised to the college practices itself. Time was also made at Senior Management Team meetings for members of the network to present their work, and the 'academic board', an opportunity for all academic staff to discuss research and other classroom facing concerns with the management teams, was re-instated at the network's request.

Outside these opportunities, the network was also able to make some limited progress towards the normalisation of research work. Initially, they were successful in re-instating the college part-funding or giving time dispensation for those undertaking master's and PhDs. However, this developed over time, and the network was a contributor to the development of the 'Research Manager' role in 2020. Unusually for the sector at the time, this was a position that aimed to support and develop initiatives within the college, including the development of internal research projects whose findings fed into college policy (Jones, 2020).

To support its members and others outside the college, a dissemination space was launched in September 2018, the Bedford College Group Research Network blog (accessible at: https://bcgresearchnetwork.wordpress.com). This was an initiative that ran for three years and published 36 blogs. It was a space to share both research projects and thoughts about research-related issues from across the sector, such as funding or Ofsted's lack of use of FE-based research in the 2019 inspection framework.

The network inspired others, first at Tresham College (see Jones, 2020) and then Sandwell (see Knott, 2021). This replication and adaption of spaces is commonplace and, as has been previously recorded, Bedford was not the first college to develop a research network. However, reflecting 10 years since its inception, the network, which still runs at the point of writing, makes a point about how to develop the much longed for FE research culture. Perhaps the most important issue is not who is first, or indeed the longevity of each innovation, perhaps instead it is the continued adaption, activity and sharing of spaces that allows the practitioner research movement to become visible to new sets of people, in new ways. If each initiative leaves its mark and adapts practice, perhaps in years to come the sector will have even more great work like the work contained in this book.

Sam Jones 10th June 2024

The Association of Research in Post-Compulsory Education

The Association for Research in Post-Compulsory Education (ARPCE) was founded around 1980, with the purpose of promoting good practice in the FE sector and, as Geoffrey Elliott notes in his foreword, was originally known as the Further Education Research Association (FERA).

Over the years, the ARPCE has run some three dozen conferences, originally focusing on policy and research. More recently, the focus has been on our biennial international research conference, which takes place in July in Oxford, at Harris Manchester College. As this book goes to press, the fifth international conference will be under way, in July 2024, with the inaugural conference having run in July 2014.

As noted in the foreword, the association between the ARPCE and the international, fully peer-reviewed journal, *Research in Post-Compulsory Education* (*RPCE*), published by Taylor and Francis, began due to Geoffrey Elliott's commitment to both, bringing together leaders in the field to report on the important work in the areas of post-compulsory education (PCE), not least vocational, work-based learning, further, higher, and adult and community education, and includes a particular focus in practitioner research.

The association is run by a voluntary committee, made up of members from across the further and higher education sectors. They welcome members from across the diversity of the post-compulsory sectors, and the membership is free, via a simple website sign-up. All ARPCE members receive free access to the internationally respected *RPCE* journal, via the website, and the editorial board welcomes articles from practitioners.

The longevity of the association demonstrates the great importance of a space for research into PCE, and the commitment for sharing good practice.

Kerry Scattergood
ARPCE committee member and RPCE referee
26 June 2024

FEResearchmeet

In November 2016, during a Learning and Skills Network meeting, it was posited aloud why weren't there more opportunities for FE practitioners to share their research (Jones et al., 2024)? There are some excellent opportunities for those interested in FE to share research, such as the Association for Research in Post-Compulsory Education (ARPCE), but the traditional style conference and journal can be intimidating for FE practitioners, being better aimed and designed for our higher education colleagues.

This isn't to suggest that FE practitioner-researchers aren't capable of sharing their work at conferences, only to suggest that these spaces have not been created for the purpose of sharing FE work and that higher education spaces are often gate-kept by the types of language used and the format of such events, such as writing abstracts and presenting papers. Moreover, these HE spaces are not designed to showcase the scope of work from across FE, such as the OTLA work funded by the Education and Training Foundation (ETF), and actually these types of work possibly wouldn't be accepted as suitable for such spaces.

What had been identified was there needed to be a more suitable space for all those in FE to meet to share and discuss their research, often research into practice, without any gatekeeping mechanisms and without feeling like we don't belong. Such a space could also become a step towards practitioners building the knowledge and competence needed to then attend and present at conferences, such as ARPCE, which is particularly welcoming to practitioners.

The first ever FEResearchmeet, which ran in June 2017, was only ever intended to be a one-off event, but it sparked something. Once others heard about the success of the event, through social media and in other spaces, other potential convenors were stepping forward to run FEResearchmeets in their own areas. Not only did this demonstrate the current interest for practice-focused research, it also suggests there was a need at this moment in time for something. This was perhaps a downstream reaction to years of performativity measures in FE: FEResearchmeets represent something more than merely interesting for practitioners, but a chance to reclaim our own autonomy and agency in our professional development. There is also an opportunity to make learning, research and development that had been invisible previously, largely existing only in the heads of those who completed the projects, to become more visible (Elliott, 1996), and hopefully utilised, across the sector.

In doing so, we argue that FE practitioner-researchers are reclaiming their own expertise. Whenever discussing this opportunity with colleagues, there is always one question on my lips: who is the expert in your classroom if it isn't you? This question helps challenge the idea that someone, somewhere else, knows better than us. It helps frame the reality that what we know about good practice, and how we come to know it, is an important aspect of knowledge-making and should not be underestimated.

Furthermore, as FEResearchmeet can be run by anyone, and it is a democratic grassroots movement, for FE by FE. Practitioner-researchers are welcome to attend, share their work or even host their own meet, with the only rule being events must be free to make them as accessible as possible. Some have been supported by other organisations to make them possible, such as the National Education Union (NEU) or the Society for Education and Training (SET), but some have been hosted in home venues on a shoe-string, to ensure interested colleagues from across the sector can attend and feel welcome. As such, these events and the attending participants are valuing a myriad of voices, with no hierarchies or even boundaries as to who is welcome. The space created, we argue, is democratic in the way that Bernstein (2000) would understand it. FEResearchmeet develops a community, within which practices develop for 'giving and receiving' towards a common goal. When we attend, we are celebrating an opportunity to share and receive each other's knowledge, a chance to analyse or understand someone else's context and practice, and make judgements as to its suitability to our own. Moreover, as professionals, our engagement with FEResearchmeet allows us to see the tensions within our practice or working lives and explore possible futures that change this.

Since those early days, FEResearchmeet, in its democratic and organic form, continues to spark, develop and grow. We believe the format has stood the test of time and hope, that in writing about – and sharing the concept of – FEResearchmeet, many others like it will follow.

Kerry Scattergood, 16 June 2024.

The Education and Training Foundation

The Education and Training Foundation (ETF) is the national workforce development body with a charitable objective to improve learner outcomes across the Further Education and Skills (FES) sector. Since its inception in 2013, it has supported a range of research activities to improve teacher pedagogy, from small-scale projects involving single departments or individuals to region-wide activities promoting change and sharing of effective practice. As the custodian of the sector's national standards in teaching, these projects have had an explicit aim to champion and disseminate research-informed practice. Two specific research programmes over the ETF's lifespan capture the essence of this ambition: the Outstanding Teaching, Learning and Assessment (OTLA) projects which ran from 2015 to 2022 and the Practitioner Research Projects (PRPs) which were undertaken in collaboration with Sunderland University between 2018 and 2023.

The OTLA projects focused on empowering practitioners to explore effective practice most helpful to their own challenges. Over 200 collaborative projects were commissioned since 2015 involving thousands of practitioners. In the Spring of 2021, Dr Lynne Taylerson undertook a thematic review into the outcomes of six OTLA projects spanning 2019 and 2020. Her analysis was framed around the concept of 'practice architectures' (Kemmis, 2017, in Powell, 2018, p. 2) which considered teachers':

- 'Doings' – the resources available in the classroom and wider environment
- 'Sayings' – their general and subject-specific language, ideas and concepts taught
- 'Relatings' – their relationships with learners, peers and support colleagues.

The OTLA projects supported the development of all three aspects of teachers' practice. In 'doings', Taylerson observed that researchers were more confident in adopting new pedagogies such as the flipped classroom, discovery learning and methods of contextualising and personalising the curriculum.

They also reported 'an increase in learner motivation and engagement following wider use of game-, problem- and project-based learning' (ETF, 2020). Furthermore, practitioners developed affectively, reframing their 'sayings' and 'relatings' around effective and empathic relationship building. Taylerson writes:

> The impacts of this new knowledge were seen in the extended use of resilience-building strategies such as the VESPA mindset programme (Oakes and Griffin, 2017). Practitioners engaged learners in discussions on self-perception and self-esteem. Dialogues on the impacts of past challenges on health and wellbeing were also held. I think a notable additional outcome is that teachers acknowledged that skills in empathetic management of sensitive discussions and ability to use empathetic vocabulary developed significantly after engaging in these discussions.
>
> (ETF, 2020)

These projects were a powerful mechanism for individual practitioners and teams to raise their professional profiles within organisations, being held synonymous with enabling experimentation and innovation, collaborative working and positive relationship-building. Fundamentally, the OTLA projects helped practitioners to 'reconnect with their enthusiasm for teaching' (ETF, 2020).

ETF's Practitioner Research Programme was delivered in partnership with the University of Sunderland's Centre of Excellence in Teacher Training (SUNCETT) and provided intensive research training and mentorship for practice-focused research at MA and MPhil Level to teachers and leaders working in the English FES system. ETF was aware of the deep-seated reservations (e.g. Lea and Simmons, 2012) reported in the literature around the sector's research culture, and existing a priori assumptions that often contested its impact, and so was determined to establish an impact narrative at the outset.

Impact was observed in several ways: PRP activity improved teaching and learning (94% of participants in 2021–2022 felt that the PRP had a positive impact on their teaching knowledge and skills, 93% reported improved confidence as a direct result of their participation and 50% took their PRP experience back to a student-facing role), it increased the sector's research capacity (the PRP trained 143 FE teachers and supported numerous cascade and dissemination events), it fostered innovation and improvement (teachers embedded new research-based methods and thinking in their classroom) and it supported individual career progression (as reported by those taking part).

In both cases, there was near unanimous agreement amongst participants that engagement with these programmes had benefited individuals *and* their organisations, through knowledge-sharing, new methodologies and improved pedagogic effectiveness, boosting researchers' professional status, while enhancing the organisation's reputation. Most striking of all was the fact that change was in the hands of practitioners, positioning research as both a force for good and a national imperative in what was seen as a 'noisy' climate where misinformation and myth about 'what works' can prevail.

Dr Paul Tully, Associate Director Membership & Business Growth,
Education and Training Foundation
24 June 2024

The Research College Group

In 2020, the Bedford College Research Manager had a conversation with colleagues about the creation of the Research Schools. It was clear that a similar funded project for the post-16 sector would not be forthcoming, so they came up with a radical idea – why not ask a number of practitioners they had already engaged with to persuade their institutions to set themselves up as Research Colleges? They contacted those individuals and the group, who came from ten different institutions across the sector, agreed to meet to discuss the idea. From that meeting of minds, the Research College Group (RCG) emanated.

The first few meetings were spent deciding upon what was meant by a Research College and what would be expected of institutions which joined the Group, how individual members from other institutions could be accommodated and how the Steering Group would operate. This resulted in the creation of a mission and vision statement called Research College Group – influencing change through research. This document was then signed by the principal of each member institution.

This document outlines the mission of the RCG as being to inform and develop practice in research from within the post-16 education and training sector, to develop the research capacity and expertise across the group of member organisations, to collaborate on research and delivery projects including those funded by third parties and to nurture expertise and confidence to empower colleagues. It defines the values of the organisation as being covered by the overarching statement 'for the sector, by the sector' and Ambition, Integrity, Respect, Curiosity and Diversity. It then outlines the vision and membership requirements for the Group.

The Steering Group then started work on the nuts and bolts of the RCG. An ethics procedure was set up, including an Ethics Committee, a Publications Team was put in place and the Group carried out data collection around the use of Digital Pedagogies within the member institutions during Covid-19 lockdowns. A regular slot was gained in the ETF's Intuition publication, and the RCG began to work with LSRN, #FEresearchmeet and the ETF to build its activities into the sector's research activities.

Almost immediately, we found ourselves working for external agencies as we began to research the needs of early career teachers in the sector and developing an early career (EC) Framework. This work was completed and presented to the Department for Education (DfE) as part of Activate

Learning's project and received well. This led to work on the GCSE Resit project reported in this publication and to work with Arts and Land-based educators. An internal group began work on creating the first internal publication based on the Digital Pedagogies project. The RCG pays practitioners for the work that they do on these projects and uses excess funds to pay for the infrastructure of the group. Sterring Group members work on a voluntary basis.

With the development of a new website which did not rely on any one institution, a strong Steering Group structure where members were cognisant of their institution's position but work collegiately to promote the best for the group, the RCG has grown to be an effective advocate within the sector. There has been considerable churn in the Sterring Group, but there is current and continued interest in joining from new member institutions and individuals.

Margaret Deborah (Debi) Saunders
19 June 2024
Founder member of the Steering Group of the RCG

Notes

1 See the evaluation at Practitioner Research Programme (PRP) – The Education and Training Foundation (et-foundation.co.uk).
2 FEDA published a report *Research in FE colleges* by Martin Johnson in 1997.
3 See Purposes & Values | Learning and Skills Research Network (wordpress.com).
4 *Collaborative research in practice: illustrated by the LSDA Regional Research Scheme* by Andrew Morris and Lin Norman was published by the Learning and Skills Research Centre, London in 2004.
5 The programme of the *R&D Toolkit* and its module materials were not published; a copy is available from the author.
6 Read the publication here: Staying with the troublemakers: A... | Association of Colleges (aoc.co.uk).

References

Bernstein, B. (2000). *Pedagogy, symbolic control, and identity: theory, research, critique.* Vol. 5. Oxford: Rowman & Littlefield.
Education and Training Foundation. (2020) *Practitioner research impacts resonate all across FE practice.* London: ETF.
Elliott, G. (1996) 'Why is research invisible in further education?', *British Educational Research Journal*, 22(1), pp. 101–111.
Jones, S. (2018) *The Bedford College Group Network: The story so far.* Available at: https://bcgresearchnetwork.wordpress.com/2018/10/17/bedford-college-group-research-network-the-story-so-far/ [Accessed 16 February 2024].
Jones, S. (2020) *The college research projects pushing for change.* Available at: https://www.tes.com/magazine/archived/college-research-projects-pushing-change/ [Accessed: 10 June 2024].
Jones, S. (2022) *Great FE Teaching: Sharing good practice.* London, SAGE / Corwin.

Jones, S., Scattergood, K., Rees, J. and Crowther N. (2024) 'FEResearchmeet. A Further Education (FE) practitioner-researcher led initiative to share and develop capacity for research and scholarship across Wales and England: analysing and theorising the period of initial development', *Research in Post-Compulsory Education*, 29(3), pp. 428–451.

Kemmis, S. (2017) in Powell, D. (2018) *Practice architectures and ecologies of practices: new ways of seeing into and making changes to teaching, learning and assessment practices*. Available at: https://www.skillsforlifenetwork.com/attachments/OTLA/A%20new%20way%20of%20seeing%20into%20TLA%201.pdf [Accessed: 24 June 2024].

Knott, N. (2021) *Making space for the voice from FE – establishing a practitioner led research network in a further education institution*. Available at: https://education-observatory.co.uk/making-space-for-the-voice-from-fe-establishing-a-practitioner-led-research-network-in-a-further-education-institution/ [Accessed: 29 May 2024].

Lea, J. and Simmons, J. (2012) 'Higher education in further education: capturing and promoting HEness', *Research in Post-Compulsory Education*, 17(2), pp. 179–193.

Lloyd, C. and Jones, S. (2018) 'Researching the sector from within: the experience of establishing a research group within an FE college', *Research in Post-Compulsory Education*, 23(1), pp. 75–93.

Part I

Developing pedagogy

Chapter 1

Changing the lens

Developing teaching practice through taking a diffractive and dialogical approach to self and peer observation

Francine Warren

1.1 Introduction

If conversations about teaching have the potential to change the way teachers think about teaching, and this can have a positive impact on their practice (Jarvis and Clark, 2020; Roxå and Mårtensson, 2009), why are we not ensuring that these opportunities are built into Initial Teacher Education (ITE) and Continuous Professional Development (CPD)? As a teacher educator in a general college of further education (FE), carrying out observations of teaching and learning (OTL) gave me the opportunity to talk to teachers about their teaching; however, I felt that they rarely had the opportunity to have those conversations with each other.

My research examines what happens if we stop trying to kill two birds with one stone by acknowledging that whilst an evaluative model of observation might have its place in ITE and a college's quality assurance process, it cannot also serve as a model for supporting pedagogical innovation (Gosling, 2002). Innovation can only happen where there is space for creativity and collaboration (Avis, 2003; Donovan, 2019), but it comes at the risk of making mistakes, and no teacher wants to make a mistake in an evaluative observation.

1.2 Research questions and or aims and objectives

The aim of my study was to offer teachers an alternative experience of observation, which moved away from an evaluative model that depends on feedback from an observer and assessed reflection, and opened up opportunities for pedagogical conversations. I asked participants to video themselves, watch their video and then share it with a peer. I wanted to give teachers the opportunity to discuss their teaching, without telling each other how they should improve, but to discuss what they had learned from watching themselves and each other, using the videos they had shared.

1.3 Positionality

I began the study because I felt that not encouraging teachers to observe their own practice and that of their peers was a wasted opportunity for meaningful development. In order to keep improving, a teacher needs to be able to experiment in their practice, to take pedagogical risks, and discuss the impact of different approaches on the learning of their students openly. However, in the current environment of performance management in education, OTL and reflection of teaching have been appropriated as performative measuring tools. Teachers frequently 'play it safe' and avoid exposing potential 'weaknesses' for fear of the negative consequences. This impacts negatively on both their development as educators and their confidence as professionals because, as discussed below, teachers are unwilling to take a pedagogical risk when they are being observed.

1.4 Using knowledge

Existing research into post-compulsory education and training (PCET) looking at the impact of neo-liberal-agendas, policy churn and policy failure reveals the negative impact of increased performativity on education and ultimately on teacher agency and confidence (Ball, 2017; Norris and Adam, 2017; O'Leary, 2020; Orr, 2020). These works have informed my understanding of the debate and concur with my own experience and the stories told by my participants. O'Leary has written extensively about OTL, detailing the detrimental impact on teaching and teachers of permitting neo-liberal agendas and performativity to inform education policy (O'Leary, 2014, 2017, 2020). Although we have ostensibly moved away from graded observations, the performative shadow of Ofsted and the audit culture continues to impact on how OTL is used in colleges, thus encouraging teachers to game the system and to 'select, develop or otherwise inflect teaching practice for observation' (Beighton and Naz, 2023, p. 7). This is not to suggest that teachers are being 'devious' or manipulating the system, rather, that the system is constructed in such a way as to demand pedagogical conformity through a restrictive, tick box approach to observation, informed by Ofsted's reliance on measurable data (Thompson and Wolstencroft, 2014). Beighton and Naz (2023) quote one of their participants, who suggests 'I think teachers are now just trained to pass observations' (p. 8). I wanted the teachers I was working with to see observations as more than just something to be endured.

A further question mark over the efficacy of the evaluative model of observation is its reliance on teacher reflection as evidence of how a teacher is improving their practice. Reflection and reflective practice have been described as ubiquitous and overused (Hébert, 2015; Myers, Smith and Tesar, 2017). Furthermore, reflection in teacher education often lacks criticality (Myers, Smith and Tesar, 2017) and has become 'formulaic' (Biesta, 2019, p. 117).

This concurred with my feeling that teachers were telling me what they thought I wanted to hear in their reflections, supported by existing research, which indicates that reflection in teacher education and development has become aligned with performativity and assessment, and become a product to be assessed (Erlandson, 2005; Tummons, 2011). I therefore introduced the concept of diffractive analysis to the participants in my research. Diffraction, like reflection, is a way of describing the behaviour of waves (light or water). Reflection occurs when waves hit a barrier and bounce back, whereas diffraction refers to the bending and spreading of waves when they encounter an obstacle (see Figure 1.1).

Proponents of diffractive thinking view reflection as focusing on sameness and mirroring what has come before (Barad, 2007; Haraway, 1992). Diffraction, on the other hand, is a 'mapping of interference' (Haraway, 1992, p. 300); it encourages us to think about the impact of difference and to see difference as something that we can learn from (Bozalek and Zembylas, 2017; Warren, 2022).

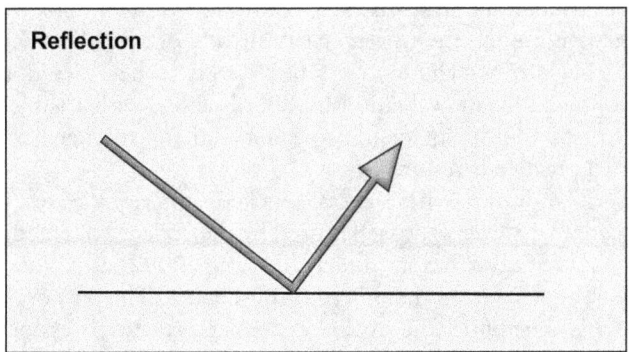

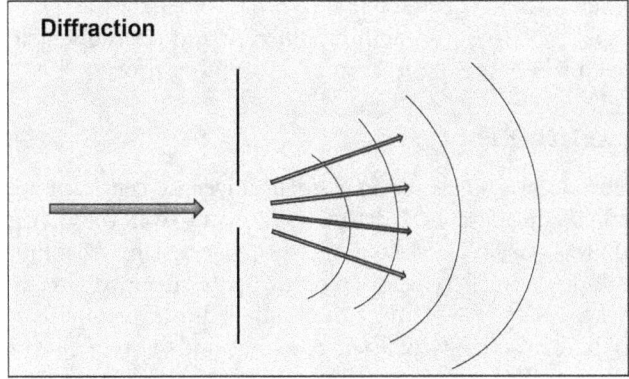

Figure 1.1 Wave behaviours (author's own illustrations)

Currently, what 'good' teaching looks like is still mandated by Ofsted. Ofsted, according to Gallagher and Smith, not only assesses evidence but 'it polices what counts as "evidence"' (Gallagher and Smith, 2018, p. 132). The impact on colleges is that 'effective pedagogy exists only in so far as it is displayed in data, spreadsheets, plans and inspection documentation' (Beighton and Naz, 2023, p. 4). Thus, observation remains a performative method by which to gauge the competence of teachers, when used in conjunction with a prescribed set of criteria, a measurable and auditable checklist. As noted above, such an approach to observation does not encourage innovative teaching or open discussion.

Too often, observation is not something that teachers have any ownership of. Where colleges use the evaluative model of observation, teachers are generally given a 'window' of when they will have a classroom visit, this is to mimic the conditions of an Ofsted visit, and they need to be prepared to impress an observer at any point in that week. Teachers are aware of the checklist the observer will be using to assess their teaching, and in my experience of being observed and observing, try to ensure that they will be seen to address those points. The conversation following the observation is almost always overshadowed by the teacher needing to know if the observer thought their teaching was good enough. It may start with 'how do you think it went?', but in the evaluative model, the observer has already decided how it went, they have ticked their boxes. The 'conversation' tends to be a description by the observee, followed by an evaluation by the observer, with a subjective list of 'what went well' and 'areas for improvement'. If the teacher has played the game, normal practice is resumed.

If the checklist does not have enough ticks in the right boxes, the teacher will be allocated whatever approach is used by the college to remedy the faults.

In his analysis of observation models, Gosling (2002) asks what is the purpose and who benefits from the different approaches. The purpose of the evaluative model is to support the quality assurance process, assess performance, provide data for appraisal, etc. This benefits the institution, not the teacher being observed (Gosling, 2002, p. 5). In order to benefit the teacher, we need to provide space for trying something different and open discussion, and this cannot happen where the observation is an auditing tool.

1.5 The existing context

The research data was collected in a small university centre of a general college of further education in Northwest England over three years. Initially, the research was part of a Master of Arts project, later becoming my doctoral research project. There were 16 participants, grouped into three cohorts of trainee teachers and one cohort of qualified and experienced teachers. All participants had experience of their teaching and written reflections being assessed and agreed to take part in a study using self and peer observation to explore their practice.

1.6 Methodology

My approach evolved over the duration of the research. The first cohort was the catalyst for adopting a diffractive approach. I had asked them to watch the videos, talk to each other about what they had seen and then to complete a questionnaire about the process. However, the questionnaire asked them how it felt giving and receiving feedback, and they used the experience as the basis for a reflective blog for their teaching qualification. This resulted in a mirroring of the evaluative observations they underwent, rather than liberating them from the performative process. By the second cohort, I had introduced the concept of diffraction and started collecting data using unstructured, one-to-one interviews with the participants.

The diffractive approach was an attempt to move teachers away from a formulaic reflection of their teaching and from giving each other feedback, I asked them to watch both their own and their peer's videos, not with a critical eye, but with an open mind. I asked them to think about the pedagogical choices that had been made, for their own teaching consider why they had made those choices, and having watched the video, consider whether they would do things differently. For their peer's video, I asked them to think about the pedagogical choices made and whether they would have made the same choices. I was explicit about the diffractive approach I wanted them to take, and that this was about asking 'why' with a view to understanding the different choices and the impact of those choices. The teachers were then asked to meet, either face to face or online, not to give feedback but to talk about the pedagogical rationale underpinning the decisions they had made in the teaching that was observed. I stressed the importance of not looking for the 'right' answer, but to look at the impact of the different choices and decisions. These pedagogical conversations were a crucial part of the process. Through conversation, we exchange ideas, begin to understand the ideas of others, and this has the power to transform our thinking, and therefore our actions (Jarvis and Clarke, 2020).

A final change to my approach was the introduction of a 'Framework for peer observation' (see Table A.1). This outlined the 'what' and the 'why' of each stage of the process and was in response to one of the participants still giving feedback to a peer.

Participation in the research was voluntary, and not all trainee teachers who were invited to take part wanted to. The cohort of qualified and experienced teachers were colleagues, and again, participation was voluntary. It was made clear at the start of the study, and through the participant information sheet that participants could withdraw at any point. I have changed the names of all participants to maintain anonymity, all names used are gender neutral, and I refer to 'they' and 'them' to further protect the participants from being identified.

1.7 Findings

My findings indicated that the teachers valued the opportunity to talk about teaching using concrete examples of practice, without being judged or asked to judge their peers. All of the participants identified something in their teaching they would like to do differently. This was not something that had been identified for them as a target, but something which came out of watching their own or another's teaching. Writing about self-observation, Lofthouse and Birmingham state that it gave the teachers the opportunity to 'engage in evidence-based studies of their own classroom practice' (Lofthouse and Birmingham, 2010, p. 15). This opportunity was amplified by also being able to watch their peers.

One of the participants, Kai, commented that having watched their own and their peer's video, they saw that they did not give the students enough thinking time after asking a question and described the conversation they had with their peer (Erin):

> we spoke about why (they) did it in the way (they) did it and what (they) hoped to achieve from that [....] So it wasn't a conversation of where I felt (they) could improve owt or anything like that. It was more like, oh, actually Erin I really liked how you did that I'm gonna use that in mine

This example of the impact of the diffractive approach I asked the teachers to take may appear to be focusing on a minor moment in the classroom. However, these are the 'small but consequential differences' (Haraway, 1992, p. 218) that exploring the impact of difference can have. The observations and conversation led to an awareness of cognitive overload and to the confidence to be able to allow thinking time and silence. As an observer, I have made these points as feedback on countless occasions; however, using their own practice and the ensuing pedagogical conversations as evidence had a far more powerful effect, which leads to changes in practice.

An important part of the process was that I was not part of the discussion, nor did I see any of the videos:

> It was about just a sharing and a conversation .... and what I liked about it too was that you hadn't asked to see any of that .... you didn't ask to see our conversation, ... so that's a safe space, isn't it?

1.8 Conclusions

When I started the project, it was based on my own experience and the feeling that observing teaching, whether your own or somebody else's, enables you to see something that a description or memory does not. But more than just watching, I felt we need to question and discuss the pedagogical choices being made in the moment – not as a judgement, but out of curiosity. Evaluative observations do not give us this freedom, there is too much pressure to do the 'right thing' and ensure we 'pass'.

Through carrying out this research, I have the confidence to challenge how observations are often used in FE colleges. Not just through my own experience, or a 'feeling' about what could support teachers to be innovative and try out different approaches. I have done empirical research that confirms for me that we cannot use observations to kill two birds with one stone. If we are saying that an observation is developmental, it cannot be part of a quality assurance process. Learning and developing are about trying out something different and considering the impact of the difference. The teachers in the project were willing to do this because they were not being judged, the purpose of the observation was clear. It was about them and their pedagogy.

Appendix

Table A.1 Framework for peer observation

What?	Why?
Getting started	
Participating in this project involves a shift away from reflecting on practice and giving feedback, to talking about teaching and asking questions about differences in practice and the choices we make when we teach.	The concept of reflection brings with it a process and vocabulary which we have become used to. It is also associated with the assessment of teaching. I want to see if there is an alternative lens through which we can view what we do. Moving away from assessment and judgement, to talking about what we do, why and asking if talking about it helps us and our students.
Groupings	
Work in groups of two to three	Smaller groups will make it manageable in terms of time and follow-up discussions.
Video self	
You might want to video a specific part of a session (introducing the session, questioning, feedback...). Or, if you're not sure, just put the video on for half an hour to see what you get.	Watching a lesson is very different from remembering what happened. Rather than reflecting on action, you see yourself in action – this can sometimes give quite surprising information.

(Continued)

Table A.1 (Continued)

What?	Why?
Watch your own video	
Watch your video – think about both you and the students. Watch for the choices you are making as you teach. Ask yourself: • Were you conscious of the choices at the time? • Do you know why you made those choices? • Would you do things differently having watched yourself? • Is there anything that surprises you or you didn't expect to see?	This is not about watching with a critical eye, more with an open mind. This gives you an opportunity to see what you and your students actually do in class, not what you think you do/remember doing. You are not watching it just to find areas to improve (although we do tend to focus on these areas initially). It is about looking back on the choices you made with those students and thinking about why.
Share your video with your partner(s)	
You can ask your partner(s) to watch a specific part of your video (give time reference) if there is something you particularly want to talk about. Or you can let them decide for themselves. If it is longer than 15 minutes, it is a good idea to give a summary of what happens so they can decide which bit to watch if they are not going to watch it all (e.g. first 10 minutes is a warmer, from minutes 17–25 questioning and feedback, etc.)	You can choose what you want to share, you are in control. You may want to discuss a particular aspect of your teaching or be happy to talk about whatever your partner has noticed. You do not need to edit the video.
Watch each other's videos	
As you are watching, consider the choices being made. • Ask why the teacher made those choices. • Are they the same choices you would have made? Remember, this is not about worse/better, just different.	Peer observation can be a great way to consider how to use different ideas and approaches. We are watching to learn, not to critique or tell others how they can improve.

(Continued)

Table A.1 (Continued)

What?	Why?
Talking about teaching	
Arrange a time to talk (F2F or online). You do not need to discuss both/all videos in one meeting, this is up to you. Discuss the questions you were asking yourself as you watched yourself and each other. The key questions are 'why' and 'what do/would I do?'	The aim is to help you to have a discussion about teaching decisions through watching yourself and others. These can be conscious or subconscious decisions, but **why** did you make them? We are not looking for the 'right' answer but looking at the impact different choices and decisions have on teaching and learning.
Finally	
As part of my research, I will arrange to interview you after you have discussed the teaching with your partner(s) to ask you how the process went. There are no right or wrong answers.	

References

Avis, J. (2003) 'Re-thinking trust in a performative culture: the case of education', *Journal of Education Policy*, 18(3), pp. 315–332.

Ball, S.J. (2017) *The education debate*. 4th edn. Bristol, UK: Policy Press.

Barad, K. (2007) *Meeting the universe halfway: quantum physics and the entanglement of matter and meaning*. Illustrated edn. Durham: Duke University Press Books.

Beighton, C. and Naz, Z. (2023) 'The calculated management of life and all that jazz: gaming quality assurance practices in English further education', *Discourse: Studies in the Cultural Politics of Education*, 44, pp. 844–858.

Biesta, G. (2019) 'How have you been? On existential reflection and thoughtful Teaching', in Webster, R.S. and Whelen, J.D. (eds.) *Rethinking reflection and ethics for teachers*. Singapore: Springer, pp. 117–130.

Bozalek, V. and Zembylas, M. (2017) 'Diffraction or reflection? Sketching the contours of two methodologies in educational research', *International Journal of Qualitative Studies in Education*, 30(2), pp. 111–127.

Donovan, C. (2019) 'Distrust by design? Conceptualising the role of trust and distrust in the development of Further Education policy and practice in England', *Research in Post-Compulsory Education*, 24(2–3), pp. 185–207.

Erlandson, P. (2005) 'The body disciplined: rewriting teaching competence and the doctrine of Reflection', *Journal of Philosophy of Education*, 39(4), pp. 661–670.

Gallagher, C. and Smith, R. (2018) 'Fear, judgement and symbolic violence', in Bennett, P. and Smith, R. (eds.) *Identity and resistance in further education*. Oxford: Routledge, pp. 129–138

Gosling, D. (2002) 'Models of Peer observation of teaching', *LTSN Generic Centre* [Preprint]. https://www.researchgate.net/publication/267687499_Models_of_Peer_Observation_of_Teaching [Accessed: 27 April 2024].

Haraway, D. (1992) 'The promises of monsters: a regenerative politics for Inappropriate/d Others', in Grossberg, L., Nelson, C. and Treichler, P. (eds.) *Cultural studies*. New York: Routledge, pp. 295–337.

Hébert, C. (2015) 'Knowing and/or experiencing: a critical examination of the reflective models of John Dewey and Donald Schön', *Reflective Practice*, 16(3), pp. 361–371.

Jarvis, J. and Clark, K. (2020) *Conversations to change teaching*. St. Albans: Critical Publishing.

Lofthouse, R. and Birmingham, P. (2010) 'The camera in the classroom: video-recording as a tool for professional development of student teachers', *TEAN Journal* [Preprint]. https://ojs.cumbria.ac.uk/index.php/TEAN/article/view/59 [Accessed: 24 April 2024].

Myers, C.Y., Smith, K.A. and Tesar, M. (2017) 'Diffracting mandates for reflective practices in teacher education and development: multiple readings from Australia, New Zealand, and the United States', *Journal of Early Childhood Teacher Education*, 38(4), pp. 279–292.

Norris, E. and Adam, R. (2017) *All change why Britain is so prone to policy reinvention, and what can be done about it*. London: Institute for Government.

O'Leary, M. (2014) *Classroom observation: a guide to the effective observation of teaching and learning*. London; New York: Routledge.

O'Leary, M. (2017) *Reclaiming lesson observation: supporting excellence in teacher learning*. London: Routledge.

O'Leary, M. (2020) 'Rethinking the improvement of teaching and learning in a virtual environment through unseen observation'.

Orr, K. (2020) 'A future for the further education sector in England', *Journal of Education and Work*, 33(7–8), pp. 507–514.

Roxå, T. and Mårtensson, K. (2009) 'Significant conversations and significant networks – exploring the backstage of the teaching arena', *Studies in Higher Education*, 34(5), pp. 547–559.

Thompson, C.A. and Wolstencroft, P. (2014) 'Give 'em the old razzle dazzle' – surviving the lesson observation process in further education', *Research in Post-Compulsory Education*, 19(3), pp. 261–275.

Tummons, J. (2011) '"It sort of feels uncomfortable": problematising the assessment of reflective practice', *Studies in Higher Education*, 36(4), pp. 471–483.

Warren, F. (2022) 'Diffracting peer observation: talking about differences, not looking for perfection', *International Journal for Academic Development*, 27(3), pp. 292–296.

Chapter 2

Shaping practice and pedagogy in offender learning

Kerry Scattergood

2.1 Introduction

I have always been passionate about reading and writing, which has become an important facet of my role as an adult literacy practitioner. I am fascinated by language and how we use it, and am interested in the relationship between literacy learning and other aspects of learners' lives, such as between the domains of work, study and home. When required to complete a small-scale research project, as part of an undergraduate course, this was an opportunity for me to deepen my understanding of literacy learning further and my first opportunity to research my own practice.

When starting out, I had an expectation that completing such a project would help inform me as a developing teacher. However, the experience of researching my own practice had far reaching ripples which I could never have predicted. Not only did the experience help me develop an aspect of my practice as a teacher but, on reflection, it also began to shape my understanding of myself as a teacher-researcher (Stenhouse, 1975). Stenhouse believes that all teachers should research their practice, thereby improving practice by 'systematically and thoughtfully testing ideas' (1975, p. 25). Here, I explore how I improved practice and further developed my identity as a practitioner researcher, through exploring an aspect of practice in an offender learning setting.

At the time of the study, I was co-ordinating a *Skills for Life* project at a large inner city probation office as part of the Offenders' Learning and Skills Service (OLASS) partnership project in England. OLASS was created in reaction to the Green Paper 'Reducing Re-Offending Through Skills and Employment: Next Steps' and the stated purpose was:

> ... ensuring offenders have the underpinning skills for life (literacy, language, numeracy and basic IT skills), and have developed work skills, (which) will enable them to meet the real needs of employers in the area where they live or will settle after their sentence is complete.
>
> (DfIUS, 2007)

Skills and employment are explicitly linked here, but the project was part of a larger ambition with other delivery strands, which included 'accommodation; drugs and alcohol; health; children and families; finance benefit and debt; and attitudes, thinking and behaviour' (DfIUS, 2007). Through this lens, learning can be seen as a step towards employment, but also part of a bigger picture in relation to offenders' lives and their place in society. Therefore, an important aspect of this work is social inclusion, a larger goal than purely employability. Adult literacy learning has long been regarded as a social justice issue (Hamilton, 2012).

2.2 Research questions and or aims and objectives

The aim of the study was to develop an understanding of everyday writing and its effectiveness with a small group of adult literacy offender learners. I had originally formed a hypothesis based on my observations of a specific group of adult literacy learners, who attended a weekly class with me at the probation office. I had identified that learners' writing could struggle to advance due to incomplete sentence structure use. However, as I began to collect the data required for my study, I identified that I was facing a greater issue because I found there was a lack of everyday writing in the learners' lives.

I wished to investigate the barriers that prevented learners from developing their writing. To enable me to do this, I asked the question:

> What does a grammatical analysis of a piece of everyday writing by my own learners reveal about its effectiveness?

2.3 Positionality

The reason I was particularly interested in focusing on offender learning was, at the time, I was involved in the probation partnership project through my role as *Skills for Life* co-ordinator and teacher. Whilst teaching adult literacy, I had observed some of the learners in the class demonstrating incomplete sentences when asked to write. On further investigation and observation, I became aware that some learners in the group were demonstrating writing anxiety (Russell, 1999) and, as a result, were not confident attempting to write in case they made mistakes. This had impacted their lives by preventing them from regularly engaging in everyday writing, thus adding to the cycle of social exclusion which could possibly include offending. Whilst the primary motivation of the study was developing pedagogy, an important motivation for me as a researcher is to promote literacy as an opportunity for social inclusion. Each individual learner's life and story matter, and building confidence and capacity through literacy learning is an opportunity for learners to value themselves and their voice.

2.4 Using knowledge

The theoretical lens used for this study was understanding literacy as a social, situated practice, as opposed to viewing literacy as a set of 'skills' remote or separate from the person and their lives. By this I mean understanding literacy and language as part of us as humans, informed by our own social, historical and cultural situations, and that is relevant to us in our lives, rather than just the remote skills of knowing where to put a full stop or how to layout a letter. A social practice approach (Barton and Hamilton, 1998; Heath, 1983; Street, 1984) to teaching adult literacy does not replace the teaching of skills but takes a wider view of literacy in the context in the learner's life (Papen, 2005). This could be within the different domains of home, study and work, plus in wider community or society activities. Furthermore, the work of Barton, Hamilton and Ivanič (2000) developed my understanding of the differences of literacies between these domains. For example, writing a note to a family member or a letter to a friend are very different practices from those enacted within a classroom setting. This became particularly significant as this cohort valued letter writing highly, to stay in touch with family or friends who were in prison.

Descriptions of language and literacy are often reduced to simplistic understandings for the sake of directing adult literacy education policy (Allatt, 2017). As such, adult literacy policy focuses on skills for employability, as was described for *Skills for Life* and now for *Functional Skills*. For example, the current suite of adult literacy qualifications, Functional Skills, are described by the Department for Education (2018) almost entirely through the lens of employability:

> Functional Skills qualifications should provide reliable evidence of a student's achievements against demanding content that is relevant to the workplace. They need to provide assessment of students' underpinning knowledge as well as their ability to apply this in different contexts. They also need to provide a foundation for progression into employment or further technical education and develop skills for everyday life.

However, this is at odds with other more nuanced views of being *functionally literate*, as is described here by the United Nations Education, Scientific and Cultural Organisation's (UNESCO, 2023) Institute for Statistics as:

> the ability to identify, interpret, create, communicate and compute, using printed and written materials associated with varying contexts. Literacy involves a continuum of learning in enabling individuals to achieve their goals, to develop their knowledge and potential, and to participate fully in their community and wider society.

This plural view (Wasik and Van Horn, 2012) of literacy incorporates literacy not only as skills for employability but as a means for developing oneself through achieving goals and developing knowledge. It expresses a broader social practice understanding of literacy than the narrower, employment-focused definition above, and such an approach has been key in developing my thinking about teaching literacy in diverse settings, such as the offender service.

In line with this understanding of literacy, this study was also particularly informed by the work of Purcell-Gates et al. (2001), who had completed a project to explore adults' changing literacy practices as a result of adult literacy education participation. There are some key learning points from this paper which it would be useful here to unpack. Purcell-Gates et al. (2001) identify the most important aspect of adult literacy education is 'the actual application of newly learned literacy skills'. Therefore, the study was designed to understand whether adult literacy learners used their newly developed skills and abilities to achieve their own goals, and to 'participate more fully in their personal and family life'. This aim can be understood, despite using the language of *skills*, as a social practice approach, as the focus is on understanding literacy in broad, pluralist terms, such as explored above. The findings of the study identified that using authentic everyday literacy texts in the classroom setting increased the likelihood of adult learners being able to apply their learning outside the classroom in their everyday lives (Purcell-Gates et al., 2001).

This is highly significant in light of the findings of the *Skills for Life* initiative. The *2011 Skills for Life Survey* reported a significant lack of progress for learners at level 1 and below, with no reported improvement in skills (Department for Business Innovation & Skills, 2012). The report identifies this effect could be due to people forgetting what they had learnt shortly after they finished their programme (Department for Business Innovation & Skills, 2012, p. 377). Here is where it becomes very relevant that adult learners are taught in a way that they are able to transfer knowledge and skills from the classroom into their own lives. Smith (2005) describes this as *mobilisation*, recognising the complexity of moving skills between domains, which describes the shortcoming identified in the *2011 Skills for Life Survey* well. This understanding also reflects the complexity of learning (Lave and Wenger, 1991), with different domains requiring a lot of learning and relearning as people do not just 'carry' their learning automatically through different domains (Tummons, 2023). Taking account of offender learners' lives became an important aspect of my project because of my developing understanding of *mobilisation*. By engaging with learners' own everyday writing completed outside of the classroom, I perceived this as an opportunity to test this out in practice.

2.5 The existing context

The class consisted of a small group of six learners, aged between 25 and 45, who attended one class a week and were enrolled on a *Skills for Life* adult literacy qualification. They had been referred to their class by their individual probation officers and had completed an initial assessment to ascertain if the class was suitable and what level of qualification they would be enrolled on.

Frankly, being offender learners, if they did not want to attend the class, then they wouldn't have, regardless of whether or not it was part of their probation requirements. The class needed to add value to their lives to be worth attending. This created an interesting situation: all the learners who attended regularly did so because they valued their learning and the class, rather than solely attending because they had to by order of the court. This was further affirmed through the data collected during the study.

2.6 Methodology

As a small class of adult literacy learners, it was entirely optional to participate. Initially, four learners agreed to participate and took part in the first stage, which was a class discussion brainstorming what everyday writing meant to us and sharing examples, plus a questionnaire to ascertain what sorts of writing learners did in their everyday lives. The discussion was videoed (due to a policy of videoing lessons within the probation office for safety purposes), which also enabled me to watch the discussion back and observe learners' reactions to the discussion. Next, all four learners were invited to submit a piece of their own everyday writing for grammatical analysis. Two learners chose to submit a piece of writing, a letter and a postcard, which were analysed for grammatical effectiveness. This stage of the project challenged my own perceptions of everyday writing, in particular in terms of the types of writing that would be important to the learners and their reasons for engaging in writing in their personal lives.

2.7 Findings

My analysis showed that learners were using quite complex grammatical techniques. Both were able to present their experiences well, putting themselves in the role of participant and demonstrating agency and effectiveness well. From the way I collected my data, I found certain anxiety demonstrated regarding everyday writing particularly a fear of making spelling or punctuation errors (Russell, 1999). However, whilst the learners might not have felt they knew the rules of spelling and punctuation, they were instinctively using grammar very effectively to suit their purpose.

This informed my pedagogy, approaching my learners' work with a greater understanding of the complexity of the effectiveness of grammar and in building learners' confidence in their writing by helping to lessen anxiety in spelling and punctuation and increasing their confidence in their own grammar use.

As importantly, I began to understand the importance of writing as part of learners' identity and as a tool for change. At the time, I also recorded that I felt research is a tool to produce change, not just for providing information (Cross, 2000). Out of my findings came a developed understanding of ways to incorporate authentic literacy tasks within the adult literacy classroom.

Furthermore, I started to understand writing better, as not only a way for adults to improve their literacy skills, but a way to explore their developing selves and to set goals (Gillespie, 1999). This is a fundamental principle that I have carried through into my more recent PhD study, exploring a social practice approach within a Functional Skills English classroom.

2.8 Conclusion

My findings were extremely useful to me in developing my pedagogy. Although at the time I felt that it was too small a study to impact my practice outside of that specific classroom, over time I have found I have generalised my learning and it has continued to shape my pedagogy. It has given me a greater understanding of everyday writing and social literacy practices, including making me aware of certain patterns, social as well as grammatical, which can cause barriers to learning. I have explored a social practice approach in a recent publication (Scattergood, 2022) where I have written about my teaching practice in a women's centre, supporting learners through their everyday writing. In the chapter, I have demonstrated how I engage learners through real-life literacy events, for example, supporting a learner to write to her MP and using this as an opportunity for learning, all of which has been a developing part of my pedagogy since completing this project.

Furthermore, this has developed out into my PhD where I am looking at the importance of stories in shaping learners' writing through their experiences, which helps adult learners in learning new ways of writing. An important aspect continues to be returning to thinking about how the classes impact people in their everyday lives, and how learning is moved from the classroom into other domains, such as the home, community or workplace.

The purpose of sharing this study, and my first steps into researching my own practice, is to demonstrate how even small-scale research projects can impact and develop thinking. Action research is often perceived as a spiral, rather than the usual cycle, spiralling outwards to not only keep impacting practice but to lead to further research and development of practitioner knowledge. To revisit Stenhouse, he also expressed that 'perhaps too much research is published to the world, too little to the village' (Stenhouse, 1981, cited in the Education and Training Foundation, 2021). I hope sharing my learning encourages others to keep sharing their research and practice.

References

Allatt, G. (2017) 'What does it mean to be literate? How the concept of 'literacy' is currently perceived by policy-makers, literacy teachers and adult learners', *Research and Practice in Adult Literacies*, 93, p. 4553.

Barton, D. and Hamilton, M. (1998) *Local literacies: reading and writing in one community*. London: Routledge.

Barton, D., Hamilton, M. and Ivanič, R. (2000) *Situated literacies: reading and writing in context*. London: Routledge.

Cross, K.P. (2000) 'The educational role of researchers', in Kezar, A. and Eckel, P. (eds.) *Moving beyond the gap between research and practice in higher education*. San Francisco: Jossey-Bass, pp. 63–74.

Department for Business Innovation & Skills. (2012) 2011 Skills for Life survey [Online]. Archived at: The National Archives. Available at 2011 skills for Life survey – GOV.UK. Available at: https://www.gov.uk/ [Accessed: 30 November 2023].

Department for Education. (2018) Subject content functional skills English [Online]. Available at: https://assets.publishing.service.gov.uk/government/uploads/system/uploads/attachment_data/file/682834/Functional_Skills_Subject_Content_English.pdf [Accessed: 22 December 2018].

Department for Innovation, University & Skills. (2007) The Offenders' Learning and Skills Service (OLASS) in England [Online]. Available at 7231-DIUS-Offender Learning Skills Service. Available at: https://www.ucl.ac.uk/ioe [Accessed: 24 April 2024].

Gillespie, M.K. (1999) Using research on writing. Focus on basics: connecting research & practice, 3:D [Online]. Available at NCSALL: https://www.ncsall.net/index.html@id=339.html [Accessed: 24 April 2024].

Hamilton, M. (2012) *Literacy and the politics of representation*. Abington, Oxon: Routledge.

Heath, S.B. (1983) *Ways With Words*. Cambridge: Cambridge University Press.

Lave, J. and Wenger, E. (1991) *Situated learning: legitimate peripheral participation*. New York: Cambridge University Press.

Papen, U. (2005) *Adult literacy as social practice: more than skills*. Oxon: Routledge.

Purcell-Gates, V., Degener, S., Jacobson, E. and Soler, M. (2001) Taking literacy skills home. Focus on basics: connecting research & practice, 4:D [Online]. Available at NCSALL: https://www.ncsall.net/index.html@id=286.html [Accessed: 13 November 2023].

Russell, M. (1999) The assumptions we make: how learners and teachers understand writing. Focus on basics: connecting research & practice, 3:D [Online]. Available at NCSALL: The assumptions we make: how learners and teachers understand writing. https://www.ncsall.net/index.html@id=336.html [Accessed: 24 April 2024].

Scattergood, K. (2022) 'Everyday writing practices for adult literacy learners', in Jones, S. (ed.) *Great FE teaching*. London: Sage, pp. 143–151.

Smith, J. (2005) 'Mobilising everyday literacy practices within the curricula', *Journal of Vocational Education and Training*, 57(3), pp. 319–334.

Stenhouse, L. (1975) *An introduction into curriculum research and development*. Oxford: Heinemann.

Street, B. (1984) *Literacy in theory and practice*. Cambridge: Cambridge University Press.

The Education and Training Foundation (ETF). (2021) *Doing action research – a guide for post-16 practitioners*. London: ETF.

Tummons, J. (2023) *Exploring communities of practice in further and adult education: apprenticeship, expertise and belonging*. Oxon: Routledge.

UNESCO. (2023) Literacy definition [Online]. Available at https://uis.unesco.org/en/glossary-term/literacy [Accessed: 30 November 2023].

Wasik, B.H. and Van Horn, B. (2012) 'The role of family literacy in society', in Wasik, B.H. (ed.) *Handbook of family literacy*, 2nd edn. New York: Routledge, pp. 3–18.

Chapter 3

Teach the Teacher

Tackling a failure mindset with GCSE resit learners in Further Education through a 'bridging the empathy gap' intervention

Rachel Arnold

3.1 Introduction

During eight years of English GCSE resit teaching in Further Education (FE), I have become accustomed to hearing learner exclamations such as 'this is too difficult', 'I will never be able to pass the exam' or 'what's the point in trying, I'm just going to fail again'. Just over a third of learners are leaving secondary school without a grade 4 pass in the essential subjects of English and Maths (JCQ, 2024), consequently finding themselves in an FE classroom attempting to face, again, the very challenge they failed to succeed in, just months before. Feelings of inadequacy, disinterest and fear frequently overcome and overwhelm these learners as they embark on their resit journey, sometimes for the third or fourth time, often resulting in disengagement. It is this space of failure I was drawn to explore, in response to too many dispiriting learner comments.

The form of my research took shape after a struggling learner earnestly expressed a request: 'I wish you could see me in the plastering workshop; it's only Maths and English I struggle with'. It was evident from this sincere interaction that my learner wanted to be recognised for what they were good at and in an environment in which they thrived. This led to the development of the 'Teach the Teacher' (TTT) intervention – an activity whereby the Maths and English teachers are taught a practical, vocational skill by the learners themselves. Built on role reversal, the Maths and English teachers attend the workshop, or another vocational space, and are put in their learners' shoes by experiencing difficulty, vulnerability and potential weakness. The learners become the experts and demonstrate confidence, knowledge and skill to teach a novice. The study explores the impact of this role reversal on the learners themselves and the extent to which it tackles the failure mindset and bridges the empathy gap.

3.2 Research questions and or aims and objectives

It was important to me to preface the study of the TTT intervention with an enquiry into how the learners really feel about having to resit their GCSE at college. I had countless anecdotal examples of their perceptions, but it seemed essential to first delve into an official line of enquiry of how the learners felt about their secondary school failure and their reacquaintance with the qualification at college.

RQ1: *What are GCSE English resit learners' perceptions of the resit course and their previous failure?*

From my own experiences in the classroom and from talking to fellow practitioners across the sector, it was evident that disengagement is a constant feature of most GCSE resit classrooms in FE. From pilot studies, I knew that the TTT intervention had the potential to positively impact learner engagement, but I wanted to know to what extent, and exactly what that looked like.

RQ2: *How does the Teach the Teacher (TTT) intervention impact learner engagement in this cohort's context?*

From the literature and the learner focus groups conducted, it was clear that positive relationships with teachers were important to the learners. Therefore, I wanted to know how the role reversal element of the TTT intervention impacted those crucial relationships. I also wanted to know whether the concept of an empathy gap was a useful lens with which to view the change in these relationships.

RQ3a: *How does the TTT intervention impact learner and teacher relationships?*

RQ3b: *In what ways could the changes between learner and teacher relationships, if any, be illuminated by the concept of 'the empathy gap'?*

3.3 Positionality

As an FE resit English teacher for eight years, my familiarity with the typical resit learner characteristics of struggle and failure affords me close proximity to the subject of the study. This can be both a threat and an advantage, when managed correctly. By being directly involved in the research, I was able to create a familiar and safe environment for the participating learners, built on trust. This is especially important due to the potentially complex topics of discussion such as personal academic failure. However, due to such a close proximity to the study, proactivity was needed to tackle biases, such as including other teachers in the study and a variety of learners. Despite having my own opinions on the resit policy, I was aware of not allowing this to dictate the trajectory of the research, and tried to disassociate the intervention with myself, so that the learners were not responding just to please me as their teacher. Therefore, despite the inevitability of my positionality interacting with the research process, I endeavoured to be as neutral as possible during the processes of collection, interpretation and presentation of data, focusing on a reflexive approach (Rowe, 2014).

3.4 Using knowledge

There are many concepts connected to the failure barrier, but the key components I explored in the existing literature included mindset theory, resilience, learner engagement and teacher-student relationships (TSRs). It is important to note that most of the literature engaging with these concepts comes from contexts outside of FE, consequently highlighting the need for more research specific to the FE context.

3.4.1 Mindset theory

The complexity of the teenage paradigm of failure is compounded by its deep childhood roots. Given that seeds of failure are often planted early, young people are often already conditioned to respond to adversity in characterised ways (Sylva, 1994). One particular study depicts the vastly different responses to failure as a result of possessing two different mindsets: helplessness and mastery (Dweck and Leggett, 1988). A helplessness mindset typically responds to challenges negatively, perceiving their difficulties as indicative of their low innate ability, convinced they were destined to fail. However, with a mastery-oriented mindset, tasks are perceived as opportunities to learn with any encountered failure seen as growth inducing and not reflective of ability. Dweck concludes that the two mindsets are not related to intelligence but are personality traits, indicative of how an individual views oneself. Dweck asserts that a helpless mindset is a fixed mindset where new things can be learned but ultimately intelligence can't be developed. Yet, a growth mindset would enable and encourage success after failure, as a form of 'expandable intelligence'(Claxton, 2002). The majority of low-level GCSE resit learners are likely to fall on the fixed, helpless mindset side of the spectrum – feeling that failure is an inevitability.

Dweck's work on mindset helps me categorise my learners, but that in itself is a form of having a 'fixed mindset'. If I label my learners as having fixed mindsets, unable to overcome the challenge of failure, and adopt resilience, then my fixed mindset could be the determining factor affecting their attainment outcome, not their own mindsets. I could be failing them from the start, especially as we know that learner outcomes are inextricably linked to mindset, both learners' and teachers' mindsets (Yeager and Dweck, 2020). Thus, I have found Dweck's mindset theory to be somewhat limiting in how I perceive my learners' abilities in the context of the resit course, but it has illuminated my thinking regarding how teacher's mindset can influence the learners' mindsets.

3.4.2 Resilience

Within the context of resit learners, resilience matters due to having to repeat a course in spite of previous failure. A useful definition of resilience is an individual's ability to 'adapt functionally and thrive during and after exposure to experiences of stress and adversity from various sources' (Bonanno, 2008, p. 2). An FE study concluded that resilience positively correlated with happiness (Short et al., 2020), and there has been significant discussion around the value of resilience and character education in supporting learner well-being in the short and long term (Duckworth et al., 2007). In reviewing the literature surrounding resilience, I was able to adopt a fresh angle by learning that it is not enough to just teach resilience in the classroom or integrate resilience education into the curriculum. Rather, regular and deliberate experiences with failure are needed, to enable a shift in perspective, whereby failure is not just something to be overcome, but something to welcome and embrace, reversing the very concept of failure as negative and impeding learning.

3.4.3 Learner engagement

GCSE resit learners in FE are typically disengaged, with low levels of self-efficacy due to repeated failure. Learner engagement is agreed to be essential to learning but also multifaceted and developmental over a learner's educational journey (Padgett et al., 2019). Studies have found that it is largely influenced by the learning environment and the support in place, or in the case of the resit learners, the occurrence of disengagement from a lack of a supported environment (Martin and Borup, 2022). It is often suggested that engagement is closely linked to a learner's enjoyment level in the classroom (Finn and Zimmer, 2012).

3.4.4 Teacher-student relationships and the 'empathy gap'

Complicated relationships with teachers have been a theme throughout their secondary school experience and is often repeated in FE too. The literature confirms that empathy is needed for positive TSRs, but there is a dearth in the literature regarding what this looks like in practice, especially for the unique FE context (Anderson and Peart, 2016). A lack of TSRs built on empathy creates significant problems, especially in FE when tackling a fixed, failure mindset (Attwood, Croll and Hamilton, 2004). A recent study highlighted the power that comes with affective and authentic empathy, in connecting learners and teachers (Maher and Morley, 2020). To achieve this authentic empathy with my learners, I need to literally be put in their shoes, and learn something unfamiliar, which does not come naturally, just as they struggle with their GCSE English resit course. My study explores the usefulness of the 'empathy gap' concept and the extent to which this can be bridged.

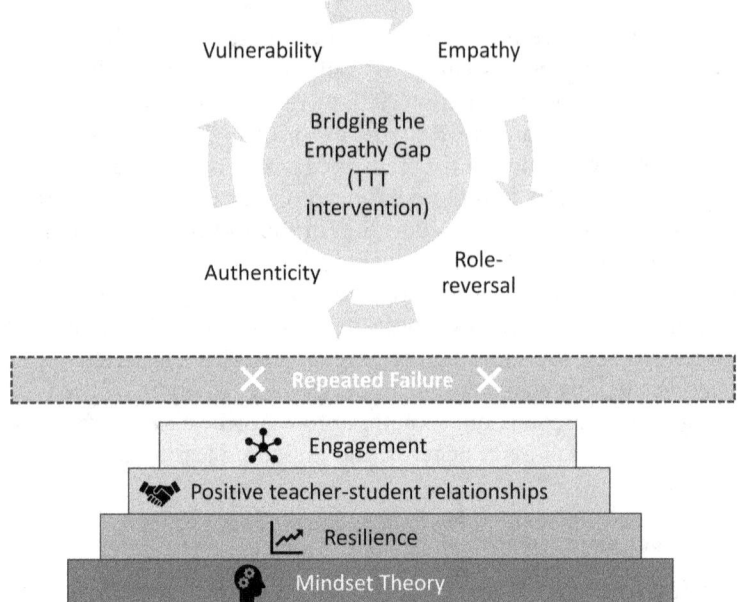

Figure 3.1 A visual representation of the conceptual framework for this study (taken from master's thesis – Arnold, 2023)

Therefore, the concepts of mindset and resilience are important foundational principles in tackling the failure barrier. However, with my learners, I am in need of a more transformative approach, whereby TSRs are not only strengthened but transformed by authenticity and empathy. Given the unique context of FE and my learners' paths, it is not realistic to expect a sudden change of mindset, or injection of resilience, resulting in a successful exam result. Therefore, the TTT intervention has been designed and studied, as a novel approach, to catalyse further research into the bridging of the empathy gap and the symbiotic nature of TSRs. It is an exploration of whether vulnerability, engagement and empathy emerge, as failure, apathy and incapability dissipate.

Figure 3.1 illustrates the foundation principles which form the composition of my conceptual framework.

3.5 The existing context

The current resit policy requires all learners in post-16 education who have not yet attained a grade 4 pass in English and maths to continue to study and work towards the qualification, as a condition of funding (DfE, 2022). This policy influences engagement in the classroom, especially for those who already have very little interest or ability in the subject. The participants are often wounded by their past failure and therefore struggle to escape the fixed, failure mindset which dictates a disengaged educational experience. GCSE English and Maths resit teaching in FE is often a replica of the secondary school model which the participants associate with failure. Therefore, the lack of a fresh and new approach can also lead to further disengagement.

3.6 Methodology

A case study of action research, in the form of a small-scale exploratory design and a qualitative methodology, was chosen to explore the research questions, focusing on two different vocational groups, two teachers and their interactions with the intervention. A combination of focus groups, semi-structured interviews and surveys were used as the methods for this design (Figure 3.2).

Within the groups, criterion-based sampling was used to select learners to participate in two focus groups (before and after the intervention) based on a variety of previous experiences and grades in English and college. Two other staff members experienced the intervention and were both interviewed individually. Ethical considerations included not taking time away from the learners' programmes of study and combining the project with their existing schedules and schemes of work. All participants were briefed, as were their parents, due to their vulnerable age.

Due to the qualitative nature of the study, most of the data gathered was from open-ended text, from the three methods used, requiring thematic analysis to triangulate the data and reduce the vast amount of open text data into workable and focused sections (Denscombe, 2017). I used NVivo to create transferable codes in order to fully analyse the data across the research questions.

3.7 Findings

RQ1: *What are GCSE English resit learners' perceptions of the resit course and their previous failure?*

The top three perceptions of the resit course included: 'fear of failure', 'waste of time/boring' and 'detrimental to mental health'. Seventy-three percent of all expressed perceptions were negative. Only one positive theme occurred in the top eight responses which recognised that the course was a 'second chance'.

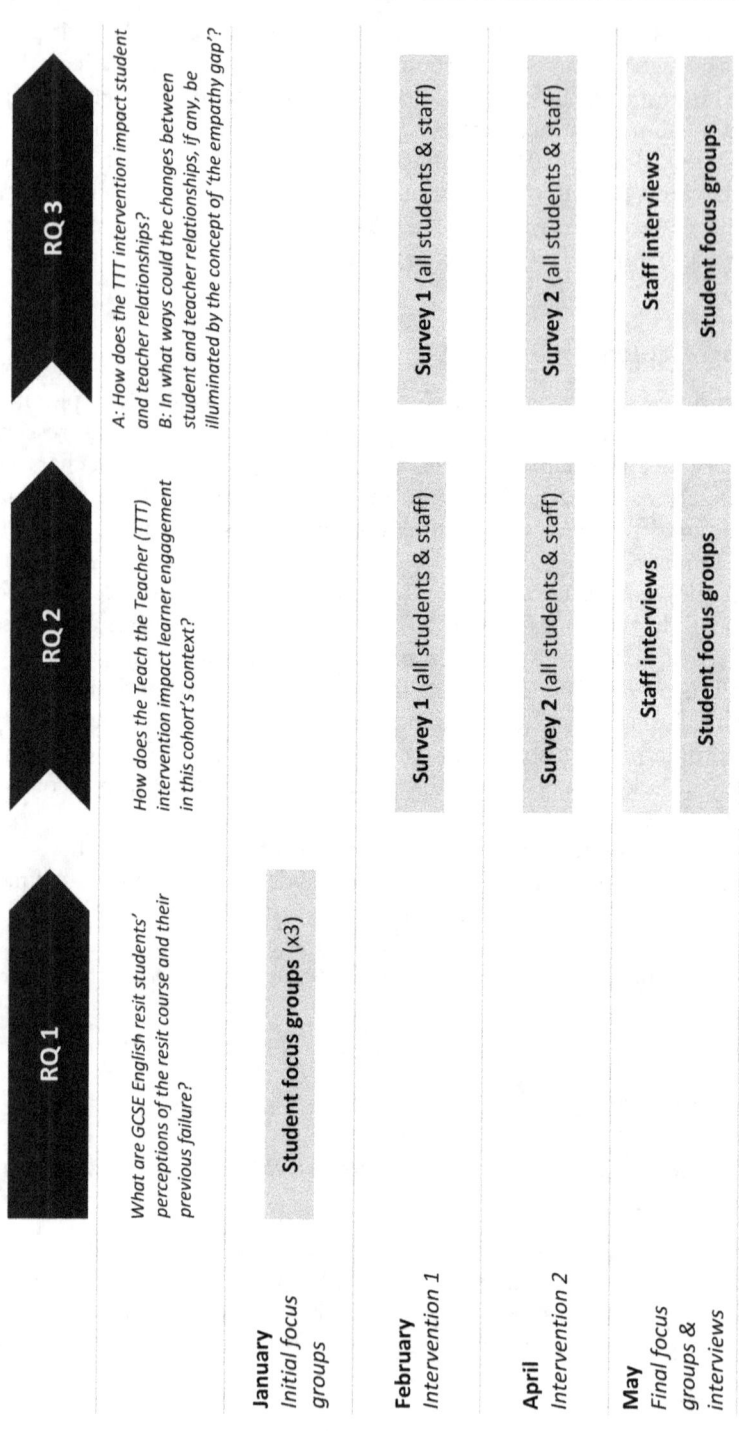

Figure 3.2 An outline of data collection methods and timeline (taken from master's thesis – Arnold, 2023)

RQ2: *How does the Teach the Teacher (TTT) intervention impact learner engagement in this cohort's context?*

There was overwhelmingly positive engagement with the intervention, with 87% of participants wanting to participate again. Learners enjoyed the role reversal element of the intervention and acknowledged feeling more confident as a result of it. They felt better about themselves due to being able to teach a novice and associated their experience with success. Proud and successful were frequent feelings after the intervention, which were also explored in the focus groups, with 'feeling good about myself' as the top emerging theme. Getting to know their teacher in a new environment was another key benefit to the activity. Interestingly, the staff perceptions correlated with the learner feedback, with the top three perceptions being: increased learner confidence, positive to see learners excelling in a different environment and positive engagement.

RQ3a: *How does the TTT intervention impact learner and teacher relationships?*

Seventy-five percent of learners felt better connected to their teachers as a result of the intervention, 77% felt better understood by their teacher and 64% felt empathy was established. Two key themes arose from the surveys, interviews and focus groups: empathy is key and the importance of investing in getting to know learners within their own comfortable environments. Importantly, the intervention positively affected relationships from both the learner and teacher perspectives.

RQ3b: *In what ways could the changes between learner and teacher relationships, if any, be illuminated by the concept of 'the empathy gap'?*

The concept of the empathy gap is useful for resit learners as it facilitates the development of new relationships, with the help of role reversal as a means of establishing empathy. The intervention helps to bridge the existing empathy gap between learners and teachers.

3.8 Conclusions

This study is an indication that by using the concept of bridging the empathy gap as a means of tackling a failure mindset, success and positive relationships can be introduced to the learners' educational experiences. The TTT intervention is a vehicle whereby positive TSRs built on empathy can be established and a failure mindset can be tackled. This is particularly important for resit learners in the FE context who are often starting their college journey from a position of 'failure'. I would use the following diagram to summarise the impact of the TTT intervention, based on the majority of the participating learners' journeys in the study (Figure 3.4).

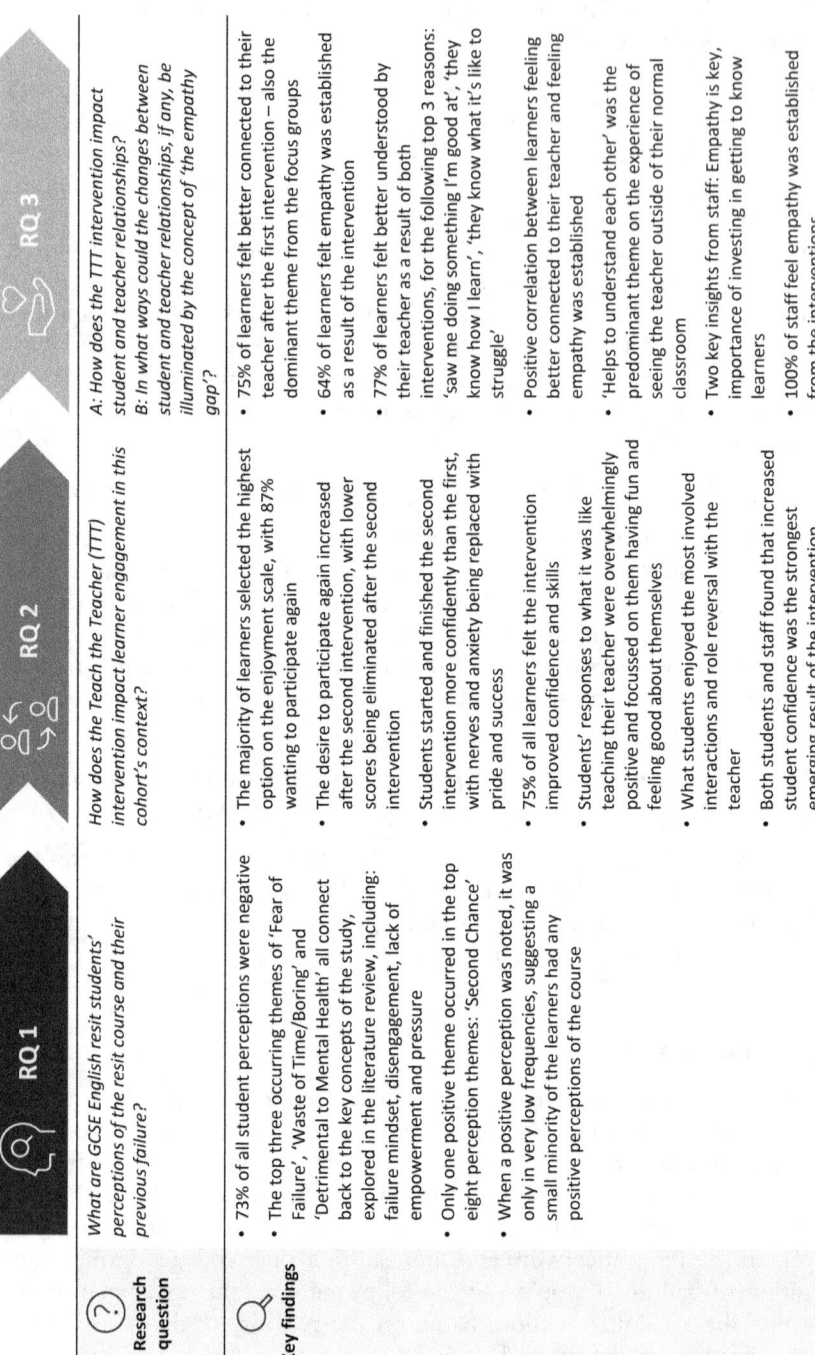

RQ 1	RQ 2	RQ 3
Research question: *What are GCSE English resit students' perceptions of the resit course and their previous failure?*	*How does the Teach the Teacher (TTT) intervention impact learner engagement in this cohort's context?*	A: *How does the TTT intervention impact student and teacher relationships?* B: *In what ways could the changes between student and teacher relationships, if any, be illuminated by the concept of the empathy gap?*
Key findings: • 73% of all student perceptions were negative • The top three occurring themes of 'Fear of Failure', 'Waste of Time/Boring' and 'Detrimental to Mental Health' all connect back to the key concepts of the study, explored in the literature review, including: failure mindset, disengagement, lack of empowerment and pressure • Only one positive theme occurred in the top eight perception themes: 'Second Chance' • When a positive perception was noted, it was only in very low frequencies, suggesting a small minority of the learners had any positive perceptions of the course	• The majority of learners selected the highest option on the enjoyment scale, with 87% wanting to participate again • The desire to participate again increased after the second intervention, with lower scores being eliminated after the second intervention • Students started and finished the second intervention more confidently than the first, with nerves and anxiety being replaced with pride and success • 75% of all learners felt the intervention improved confidence and skills • Students' responses to what it was like teaching their teacher were overwhelmingly positive and focussed on them having fun and feeling good about themselves • What students enjoyed the most involved interactions and role reversal with the teacher • Both students and staff found that increased student confidence was the strongest emerging result of the intervention	• 75% of learners felt better connected to their teacher after the first intervention – also the dominant theme from the focus groups • 64% of learners felt empathy was established as a result of the intervention • 77% of learners felt better understood by their teacher as a result of both interventions, for the following top 3 reasons: 'saw me doing something I'm good at', 'they know how I learn', 'they know what it's like to struggle' • Positive correlation between learners feeling better connected to their teacher and feeling empathy was established • 'Helps to understand each other' was the predominant theme on the experience of seeing the teacher outside of their normal classroom • Two key insights from staff: Empathy is key, importance of investing in getting to know learners • 100% of staff feel empathy was established from the interventions

Figure 3.3 A summary of key findings for each research question (taken from master's thesis – Arnold, 2023)

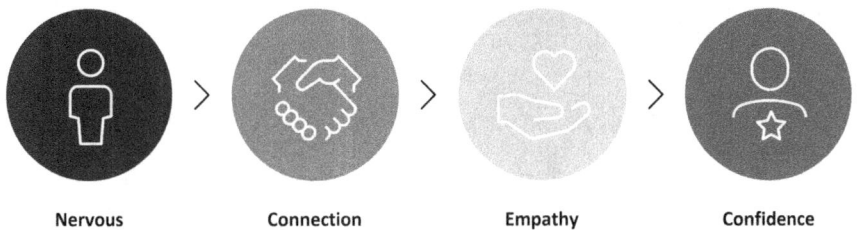

Figure 3.4 Graphic created to depict the result of bridging the empathy gap (taken from master's thesis – Arnold, 2023)

It is important to note that role reversal was a key mechanism involved in creating an environment whereby TSRs were strengthened and empathy was established and activated. These findings may be useful to any practitioner struggling to engage learners, especially learners who have experienced failure previously and are trying to progress within the FE context. Or even, any practitioner trying to progress their learners from a position of nervousness and failure towards confidence and success. As a result of these findings, my recommendations to any practitioner working with resit learners would be to find and foster opportunities to connect and build empathy and to relinquish the traditional teacher role when needed. The impact of role reversal was powerful for both the teachers and learners in this study. However, role reversal can take place in smaller ways in everyday classroom scenarios, and this should be encouraged. The findings from this study were so illuminating they led me to embark upon a PhD where I am currently exploring the impact of the TTT intervention in numerous FE colleges across England and Wales. As this was a small-scale study, it is important to examine the impact across a much larger group of participants and colleges with different cohorts. I am excited to continue this research further and hopefully move one step closer to empowering our GCSE resit learners, even beyond the four walls of the FE classroom.

References

Anderson, N. and Peart, S. (2016) 'Back on track: exploring how a further education college re-motivates learners to re-sit previously failed qualifications at GCSE', *Research in Post-Compulsory Education*, 21(3), pp. 196–213. https://doi.org/10.1080/13596748.2016.1196978

Arnold, R. (2023) *Teach the teacher: tackling a failure mindset with GCSE Resit learners in further education through a novel 'bridging the empathy gap' Intervention*. Unpublished dissertation. Cambridge, England.

Attwood, G., Croll, P. and Hamilton, J. (2004) 'Challenging learners in further education: themes arising from a study of innovative FE provision for excluded and disaffected young people', *Journal of Further and Higher Education*, 28(1), pp. 107–119. https://doi.org/10.1080/0309877032000161850

Bonanno, G.A. (2008) 'Loss, trauma, and human resilience: have we underestimated the human capacity to thrive after extremely aversive events?', *Psychological Trauma: Theory, Research, Practice, and Policy*, S(1), pp. 101–113. https://doi.org/10.1037/1942-9681.S.1.101

Claxton, G. (2002) *Building learning power: helping young people become better learners*. Bristol: TLO.

Denscombe, M. (2017). *The good research guide: for small-scale social research projects*. 6th edn. London: Open University Press.

DfE. (2022). 16 to 19 funding: Maths and English condition of funding – GOV.UK [Online]. Available at: https://www.gov.uk/guidance/16-to-19-funding-maths-and-english-condition-of-funding [Accessed: 26 March 2024]

Duckworth, A.L., Peterson, C., Matthews, M.D. and Kelly, D.R. (2007) 'Grit: perseverance and passion for long-term goals', *Journal of Personality and Social Psychology*, 92(6), pp. 1087–1101. https://doi.org/10.1037/0022-3514.92.6.1087

Dweck, C.S. and Leggett, E.L. (1988) 'A social-cognitive approach to motivation and personality', *Psychological Review*, 95(2), pp. 256–273. https://doi.org/10.1037/0033-295X.95.2.256

Finn, J.D. and Zimmer, K.S. (2012) 'Learner engagement: what is it? Why does it matter?' in Christenson, S.L., Reschly, A.L., and Wylie, C. (eds.) *Handbook of research on learner engagement*. Boston, MA: Springer US, pp. 97–131. https://doi.org/10.1007/978-1-4614-2018-7_5

JCQ. (2024) Examination results: GCSE Summer 2024. Available at: https://www.jcq.org.uk/gcse-level-1-and-level-2-results-summer-2024/ [Accessed 24 October 2024].

Maher, A.J. and Morley, D. (2020) 'The self stepping into the shoes of the other: understanding and developing self-perceptions of empathy among prospective physical education teachers through a special school placement', *European Physical Education Review*, 26(4), pp. 848–864. https://doi.org/10.1177/1356336X19890365

Martin, F. and Borup, J. (2022) 'Online learner engagement: conceptual definitions, research themes, and supportive practices', *Educational Psychologist*, 57(3), pp. 162–177. https://doi.org/10.1080/00461520.2022.2089147

Padgett, J., Cristancho, S., Lingard, L., Cherry, R. and Haji, F. (2019). Engagement: what is it good for? The role of learner engagement in healthcare simulation contexts. *Advances in Health Sciences Education*, 24, pp. 811–825. https://doi.org/10.1007/s10459-018-9865-7

Rowe, W. (2014). 'Positionality', in Coghlan, D. and Brydon-Miller, M (eds.) *The SAGE encyclopedia of action research*. Vol. 2. Thousand Oaks, CA: Sage, pp. 627–628.

Short, C.A., Barnes, S., Carson, J.F. and Platt, I. (2020) 'Happiness as a predictor of resilience in learners at a further education college', *Journal of Further & Higher Education*, 44(2), pp. 170–184. https://doi.org/10.1080/0309877X.2018.1527021

Sylva, K. (1994) 'School influences on children's development', *Journal of Child Psychology and Psychiatry*, 35(1), pp. 135–170. https://doi.org/10.1111/j.1469-7610.1994.tb01135.x

Yeager, D.S. and Dweck, C.S. (2020) 'What can be learned from growth mindset controversies?', *American Psychologist*, 75(9), pp. 1269–1284. https://doi.org/10.1037/amp0000794

Chapter 4

Investigating the teaching of agriculture in Further Education in England

Catherine Lloyd

4.1 Introduction

Having worked in the land-based sector since 1996, I have an interest in the leadership and development of land-based subjects. This led me to undertake a Doctorate in Education, which I completed in 2018 and since then I have continued to look for opportunities to undertake research, either through projects or in collaboration with others researching the sector. My current role includes line management of those responsible for practical resources, which includes a college farm. Therefore, I wanted to better understand agriculture provision and the factors which influenced curriculum delivery. It became clear that research in this area was lacking, and this motivated me to undertake a study to gain insight into this specialist subject area.

The study focused on agriculture in Further Education (FE) in England. Students enrolling on these courses are in post-16 education and studying at a specialist land-based college which may be independent or have merged with a general FE college. Land-based colleges are located in rural settings and have diverse physical resources to deliver the curriculum. This includes commercially run farms, with arable and livestock enterprises which reflect the type of farming prevalent in the region in which they are located. Courses are available at levels one, two and three (with level two equivalent to GCSE and level three equivalent to A level) and focus on production agriculture, that is the skills and knowledge required for farming.

4.2 Research questions

The purpose of the study was to investigate the teaching of agriculture in FE. The intention was to obtain and interpret the views of those delivering agriculture including the pedagogical approach taken, that is the decisions made about what and how to teach and the factors which influence these. It was set against a backdrop of considerable change within the agricultural sector driven both by government policy and environmental issues. In light of this, the project also explored whether this change was impacting the delivery of

DOI: 10.4324/9781003505389-7

agricultural education. The project had two research questions which were as follows:

1 What pedagogical approaches are used by lecturers delivering agricultural education in English FE colleges?
2 What impact are the current changes in the agricultural sector having on teaching practice?

4.3 Positionality

My intention with the research was to understand practice, not to make a judgement on its effectiveness. Whilst I work within the sector under investigation, the research couldn't be considered 'close-to-practice' (Kelchtermans, 2021) as the work was not collaborative and the research questions were defined by myself, with no input from practitioners.

I considered myself to be both an insider and an outsider in regard to the research. My background in the land-based sector was of benefit in understanding some of the contextual factors, but I was not considered a practitioner as I have not taught agriculture. Despite familiarity with the context, it is important to remain open to new knowledge and ideas. I therefore chose to recruit participants from colleges across England, to ensure the research was not too narrow in its focus and to enable me to compare and contrast views and experiences.

The research is situated within an interpretivist paradigm. At a basic level, a paradigm is a set of ideas or beliefs that underpins the theories and methodology of a particular discipline (O'Leary, 2013). The interpretivist paradigm asserts that reality is subjective and constructed by individuals based on experiences; the aim is therefore to understand the phenomenon being investigated from the perspective of those involved (Thomas, 2013). This is commonly done using qualitative methods such as interviews, focus groups and observations. The aim of my study is to understand practice. Therefore, to address the research questions, this research is a qualitative study, with an interpretivist perspective, which used interviews to obtain in-depth accounts of lecturers' experiences of teaching agriculture.

4.4 Using knowledge

It has been widely acknowledged that the FE sector is significantly under-researched with land-based subjects receiving very little attention in the literature. This study focused on pedagogical approaches to teaching agriculture. There have been several reviews on what makes good vocational teaching in FE (for example: Lucas, Spencer and Claxton, 2012). Whilst it is possible to theorise about what works in the delivery of agricultural education by drawing on studies of vocational pedagogy and subject specialist pedagogy (for example: Hanley et al., 2018), to gain further insight into practice, empirical studies are needed. These are studies which generate knowledge from experience, using real-world evidence during the investigation. As Kelchtermans (2021, p. 1054) observes, 'teaching – or more broadly educating – happens in and through practices'; therefore, descriptive accounts from practitioners can provide useful insight into the process.

As the research evidence relating to agriculture teaching was limited, I broadened my literature search to include countries outside the UK and settings such as secondary and higher education. This provided useful insight but lacked the specific contextual factors of the English FE system. I also looked at other subject areas, in particular science education as I considered that this may provide useful insight into the teaching of agriculture.

For the purpose of this chapter, I will focus on one aspect of the literature review and explain how this influenced the study. One concept which informed my thinking and helped frame the investigation was pedagogical content knowledge (PCK) (Shulman, 1987). Shulman identified seven categories of knowledge; the one of particular relevance to this study is the concept of pedagogical content knowledge, referred to by Kind (2009, p. 170) as 'the knowledge teachers use in the process of teaching'.

Kind (2009) reviewed research on PCK in science education, to better understand teachers' professional practice. The review identified features which contributed to teacher development, one of which was knowledge of the subject matter. This led me to consider agriculture as a subject and the types of knowledge and skills that it comprises. It draws from many areas and comprises both scientific knowledge and context-specific tacit knowledge, that is farmers' knowledge of the land and farming practice obtained through experience. This knowledge is combined with practical skills required to perform the tasks required in everyday farming. Teachers will draw on their subject knowledge when devising ways to teach the material so that students will understand it, a process which involves bringing together subject and pedagogical knowledge as they identify what works in promoting student learning. With experience, teachers will also begin to understand more about students' learning and the areas within the subject which may cause difficulties (Brown, Friedrichsen and Abell, 2013). This influences the way they present the content to the students.

The interview questions used in the study arose from my reading of the literature, for example, the research on areas of the subject which may cause difficulties led to the interview question: 'Are there common areas of misunderstanding in the subject and how do you address these?' I will return to this question when considering the findings of the study.

4.5 The existing context

There were a number of external factors that I felt were of relevance to the study. Agriculture both in England and globally is facing a period of uncertainty and change as it adapts to environmental issues in the face of the need to increase food production. In England, the change is driven by government policy and the legislative framework for the new regime, the Agriculture Act, was passed in November 2020. These changes in policy broadly aim to promote a transition to methods of farming which are sustainable and benefit the environment. These changes will impact all farms, including college farms used by staff and students in the delivery of the agricultural curriculum. At the time of the study in 2022, these changes were in the early stages. I wanted to explore whether this sector change was having an impact on teaching staff and their practice.

4.6 Methodology

As previously mentioned, the research was a qualitative study within an interpretivist perspective, focusing on in-depth accounts of lecturers' experiences of teaching agriculture. Critics of this method consider that the focus on words and meaning rather than numerical data means it lacks rigour. To address this, it is important that the research is carried out in a systematic way and that transparent and clear descriptions of the research process are included. One way to evaluate research is to consider whether it is trustworthy. The aim of trustworthiness in qualitative inquiry is to support the argument that the inquiry's findings are 'worth taking account of' Lincoln and Guba (1985, p. 290). They identify four features of trustworthiness: credibility, transferability, dependability and confirmability which can be considered when reflecting on your methodology and approach.

To carry out the study, I needed to gain access to individuals teaching agriculture in FE. I used established networks within land-based colleges and emailed details of the study to key contacts asking them to pass it on to relevant staff. In total, 23 individuals responded, which resulted in 17 interviews. This method is purposive sampling, as I identified the group of people who were most likely to be able to help answer the research questions and asked for volunteers. This approach can be problematic as those who come forward to take part are likely to have an interest in the topic under investigation and this could impact results. Therefore, care should be taken not to assume that the results are representative of all agriculture teachers.

Ethical approval was obtained from the university supervising the project. In this study, the participants were adults, and having been provided with written information about the purposes of the research, they were able to give informed consent. I provided the participants with a list of interview questions in advance to help them decide whether or not to take part. I made them aware that their words may be quoted but that I would provide anonymity by using pseudonyms which would enable me to distinguish participants but not reveal their identity.

Semi-structured interviews formed the principal means of gathering information and time was spent devising the questions to ensure they would provide information relevant to the research objectives. The interviews comprised 12 questions, starting with participants' background and experiences, moving on to approaches to teaching and impact of changes in the sector on practice. This format allowed me to keep the interviews on track but also to add relevant follow-up questions if appropriate. The interviews were conducted over Microsoft Teams and were recorded and fully transcribed. After each interview, I noted down my initial thoughts, which started to build a picture of the issues raised by participants. Once the interviews were complete, I used software to help in the analysis. To do this, I used constant comparative analysis (Fram, 2013), and this involves systematically going through the data comparing the elements and looking for areas of agreement and difference. The process of coding involves grouping words or phrases that arise from the transcripts together into themes. As the process progresses, there may be a decline in the number of new themes being identified. Data saturation is the point at which additional data doesn't provide new insights or aid in building theories (O'Leary, 2013). It is the researchers' job to identify when saturation has been reached, then to interpret the data and decide whether it sheds light on the research questions under consideration.

Participants were given the opportunity to comment both on their transcript and on a summary of the themes identified from the data. This can increase the credibility of the researchers' interpretation of the data and in turn the trustworthiness of the study.

4.7 Findings

The participants' teaching experience varied from 1 to 20 years, and they all had experience of agriculture either through farming or working in related industries. In regard to the pedagogical approach taken by lecturers, there was consensus among the participants despite their varying length of experience and being located in different colleges, which gives some confidence in the findings. I identified a number of themes from the data and presented these using quotes from the participants. The quotes give a feel for the themes, but it must be remembered that they are from individuals and may not represent the whole group.

To illustrate this, I am going to draw on the responses to the interview question presented earlier which are related to common areas of misunderstanding.

Seven of the 17 participants identified a particular subject, plant and soil science as a topic which students were more likely to find challenging and may have difficulty understanding some of the content. This was evidenced in comments made by participants, who also offered reasons why this might be the case:

> It is those more science based subjects I think, that have the issue
>
> (Emma)

> They just kind of they switch off from the science stuff, a lot of them have already been disengaged at school with it
>
> (Henry)

> Plant and soil science, very often it is because it wasn't their strength at school
>
> (Anne)

The suggestion is that for some learners, their prior experience of the subject may impact how they engage with it at college. Other participants described how because of this, it was important to assess students' starting points, in order to move forward:

> …science knowledge, you know there are real gaps there sometimes
>
> (Helen)

> I'm just reaffirming that the starting point is correct and then I build on it that
>
> (Ethan)

In terms of addressing this issue, many of the participants referred to making the content as relevant and as practical as possible by incorporating into activities that students could engage with. The following quotes highlight this:

> Getting across the relevance and the understanding of how important that is to them
>
> (Emma)

> Make it as applied as possible trying to do as many experiments as possible
>
> (Anne)

The participants quoted here have identified subject content which may cause difficulties, and this has influenced how they present it to the students. This highlights the importance of talking to practitioners about what they know and how it influences their decisions about what and how to teach. Brown, Friedrichsen and Abell (2013) describe how this understanding develops as the teacher becomes more experienced which can be seen in a very honest quote from one of the participants:

> I didn't get that right to begin with. I just started on and assumed they got it and soon realized they weren't getting any of it.
>
> (Adam)

The literature is useful in helping to interpret the participant responses and identifying themes for further exploration. Through this, you can identify whether the findings are relevant in helping to answer the research questions.

4.8 Conclusions

In conclusion, the overall findings of the study did assist in answering the research questions posed at the start. I was able to describe features of the pedagogical approach taken to teaching agriculture in FE and put forward some suggestions as to how the changes in the agricultural sector were influencing practice.

It is important to note the limitations of the study; I only used one method of data collection, semi-structured interviews and what people say they do might be different from what they actually do. Trustworthiness would be increased if I had supplemented this with other methods such as observations to provide further insights into practice. The study was small scale, comprising only 17 participants and therefore cannot be said to be representative of the whole population, so caution should be taken in extrapolating the results. Through providing a detailed description of the research process, readers will be able to judge the trustworthiness of the study (Lincoln and Guba, 1985).

There are many areas for future research to add to this subject area and expand the body of literature from which others can draw. This could include collaborative research with practitioners, action research projects and inclusion of a wider range of participants such as students to give another perspective.

Kelchtermans (2021) identifies that if research is to be meaningful for practice, it needs to be communicated and shared. Conscious of this, I set out to present my findings to a range of different audiences, which involved presenting at conferences and subject specialist events. I published my findings in a journal (Lloyd, 2023) and in a number of think pieces (AoC Think Further). The purpose of the study was to better understand the teaching of agriculture, not to measure its effectiveness or inform practice. Through shining a light on this under researched area, I hope that individuals will reflect on its relevance to their setting, as a practitioner in agriculture, in a related land-based subject or in another vocational area.

The research discussed in this chapter was supported by Research Further, the scholarship project run by the Association of Colleges in partnership with NCFE.

References

Brown, P., Friedrichsen, P. and Abell, S. (2013) 'The development of prospective secondary biology teachers PCK', *Journal of Science Teacher Education*, 24(1), pp. 133–155.

Fram, S.M. (2013) 'The constant comparative analysis method outside of grounded theory', *Qualitative Report*, 18(1), pp. 1–25.

Hanley, P., Hepworth, J., Orr, K. and Thompson, R. (2018) *Literature review of subject-specialist pedagogy*. London: Gatsby.

Kelchtermans, G. (2021) 'Keeping educational research close to practice', *British Educational Research Journal*, 47(6), pp. 1504–1511.

Kind, V. (2009) 'Pedagogical content knowledge in science education: perspectives and potential for progress', *Studies in Science Education*, 45(2), pp. 169–204.

Lincoln, Y.S. and Guba, E.G. (1985) *Naturalistic inquiry*. London: Sage.

Lloyd, C. (2023) '"Not just go into a field to turn the soil over, they've got to understand the science behind it." Using pedagogic content knowledge to uncover teaching practice in agriculture', *Research in Post-Compulsory Education*, 28(2), pp. 295–312.

Lucas, B., Spencer, E. and Claxton, G. 2012. How to teach vocational education: a theory of vocational pedagogy [Online]. Available at: https://www.improving-technicaleducation.org.uk/assets/__/resource-library/resource/pdf/report-how-to-teach-vocational-education.pdf [Accessed: 12 December 2023].

O'Leary, Z. (2013) *The essential guide to doing your research project*. London: Sage Publications.

Shulman, L.S. (1987) 'Knowledge and teaching: foundations of the new reform', *Harvard Educational Review*, 57, pp. 1–22.

Thomas, G. (2013) *How to do your research project: a guide for students in education and applied social sciences*. London: Sage Publications.

Part II

Overcoming barriers in the sector

Chapter 5

Reducing barriers to learning opportunities for healthcare professionals to improve attendance

Katie Barrett

5.1 Introduction

Firstly, a disclaimer that I'm no researcher, and this research was born out of a small action research project whilst undertaking a Post Graduate Certificate in Education (PGCE). Secondly, I've never published work or written a book chapter before. All firsts for me. The research outlined in this chapter challenged my view of what's achievable and possible and demonstrated that small actions can have a big impact. Undertaking the research outlined in this chapter showed me that research isn't scary, unobtainable, a complex entity or something only people with doctorates engage in. It's accessible and applicable for everyone and can be applied to anything, big or small.

To give context, I'm a psychotherapist working within the NHS managing support and counselling services. My area of expertise relates to death and dying, and supporting patients and families diagnosed with life-limiting illnesses and cancer. I've worked in the NHS all my working life and have 20 years of experience working within this complex and multi-faceted organisation in both Wales and England, from a hotel services role after school, nursing roles, therapist, to my current managerial role.

5.2 Positionality

This action research project was born from my personal experiences and a passion for the role education plays in developing professional and clinical practice. Healthcare professionals dedicate a vast amount of time, energy and commitment to their profession, many requiring intense study to undertake their roles. However, within the NHS, there are limited opportunities to engage in learning opportunities that encourage reflective practice, particularly around the sensitivity of how to emotionally and psychological support patients and bereaved families. There's an assumption that those in clinical roles automatically have the skills and knowledge to effectively support patients and families in an effective way; however, supporting patients nearing end of life and bereaved families is a skill that requires refining like the many other skills healthcare professionals develop. This often leaves healthcare professionals in challenging and difficult situations where they are expected to provide a high level of psychological support and care during highly emotive and distressing situations where they have had very little training or support on how to do this. Naturally, many healthcare professionals fear or avoid these situations, not out of lack of care or compassion, but due to lack of confidence or 'fear of saying the wrong thing'. The stress and fatigue of managing work life balance leaves many healthcare professionals depleted and emotionally burnt-out. Education can support healthcare professionals' ability to build resilience, boundaries and prioritise themselves to care for others, which is vital in promoting longevity in these demanding and stressful roles.

5.3 Research question and current context

I've never expected to have undertaken a teaching qualification or had much interest in teaching but have consistently engaged in higher education throughout my working life and value the role education has played in my professional and personal development. I was provided an opportunity to undertake a PGCE to underpin the work I was already doing providing psychoeducation to healthcare professionals within my role, and this opportunity felt like a gift, and I feel passionate about passing this knowledge and gift on to others.

Whilst gaining the required teaching hours for my PGCE, it was apparent that healthcare professionals were struggling to attend teaching sessions. It was important for me to pay attention to this as it was demonstrating clearly that staff were struggling to attend, and this seemed significant because not only could this information inform my teaching practice but also highlight what support may be needed to help staff engage in learning opportunities (Oldfield et al., 2019). I know from personal experience that attending training opportunities is extremely difficult due to staff shortages, sickness, and lack of funding or resources, so this was of no surprise. Non-attendance can have a detrimental impact not only on the individual's professional development but on the workforce too as it reduces opportunities to develop desirable skills within teams and can negatively impact morale. The recognition of this issue and experiencing the challenges from the other side as an educator trying to encourage attendance informed my small action research project and led me to my research question, *how can reducing the barriers to learning opportunities improve attendance rates for healthcare professionals?*

The aim of my research was to discover the challenges healthcare professionals were facing, especially in a post-covid era where digital advancements within the NHS has provided more accessibility, cost-effective ways to engage in learning, and challenged many of the previous barriers such as increased travel time due to rurality and reduced clinical time with patients (Lumsden, Byrne-Davis and Scott, 2020). Being passionate about education and having lived experience as outlined above, I was personally invested in my action research project. I was curious to explore, test and find a solution to the universal challenges healthcare professionals encounter when accessing learning opportunities. My bias and passion often needed to be kept in check to ensure my personal experiences, thoughts, beliefs and passion were metaphorically locked away in a box to not inform or influence the research.

5.4 Existing knowledge

Conducting the literature review was an important process for me, especially recognising the need to manage my personal bias and provide an opportunity to build knowledge and perspective on this topic area which may challenge my own personal views and experiences. I used a repetitive process to identify relevant research to conduct a comparative analysis and used three major databases to trace literature related to healthcare education, searching terms such as 'healthcare learning' and 'non-attendance'. This was consciously decided to restrict the search hits which could have been overwhelming and maintain a sense of focus.

For the interest of conducting this small-scale research that would hopefully have value, purpose and be achievable to undertake, I decided to focus on three dominant themes that presented across all research papers I reviewed, study leave, workload and leadership. Research demonstrated that healthcare professionals attending training could benefit patients directly, and research by Holland et al. (2019) demonstrated that workload had a direct impact on nurse's mental health and well-being, and subsequently on job satisfaction and work-life balance. Further illustrating that proactive, supportive management encourages staff to engage in high involvement work practices which can increase job satisfaction.

The importance of managerial support was further reinforced by Ramani, McMahon and Armstrong (2019). This research identified that leaders have a pivotal role in promoting learning principles, alongside identifying and overcoming system barriers to change, further outlining the importance of developing and maintaining learning programs to support this, paying attention to tailored program design, implementation and evaluation. This is something I have since taken away and adopted into my practice when considering delivering teaching to healthcare professionals. It must be of value to the attendees, relevant, effective and provide restorative learning experiences tailored to individual needs in an ever-changing healthcare climate.

Coventry, Maslin-Prothero and Smith (2015) demonstrated that the consequences of ineffective management and leadership increase workload and staffing issues, which directly impacts clinical practice competency, provision of quality patient care, job satisfaction and retention of staff. Further suggesting that supportive leadership offered a solution, and from my own personal experiences, I believe there's a positive correlation between education and improving patient outcomes.

Although there was research on the benefits of staff engaging in learning opportunities, there is very little research on the implementation of change in counteracting some of the barriers identified. I recognised from the literature review that management played a key role, that effective and supportive management could offer solutions to some of the other barriers faced as outlined.

5.5 Methodology

Due to the nature of the taught subject matter on death and dying, it was most appropriate to undertake the research from a person-centred, humanistic stance and adopt an interpretivism approach. This was fundamental to facilitate healthcare professionals to share their experiences and 'to understand the subjective world of their experience' (Cohen, Manion and Morrison, 2018, p. 17).

On reflection, I recognise my bias here as this is a comfortable positionality for me to adopt as a self-proclaimed humanistic therapist. I'm curious to consider if I'd adopted a scientific or systemic approach grounded in standards and procedures, what would have transpired. However, delivering experiential workshops to healthcare professionals where self-reflection is facilitated by their nature is subject to change. No bereavement, grief and loss workshop are ever the same due to the participants' interaction and sharing of their subjective experiences and attitudes towards the subject. However, I needed to be realistic in what was achievable when delivering these teaching sessions online in an NHS context which is challenging and ever changing. I also needed to acknowledge the ethical considerations. For example, all feedback was anonymous, with no identifiable information, and needed to consider the impact on attendees given the taught subject matter and that I may need to provide further support if needed. Controlling the environment or external factors just would not be achievable. Adopting interpretivism is grounded in using the individual's reported experiences and understanding as data where theory and insight can be generated to support and promote learning opportunities by identifying the barriers faced, and this would require several data cycles.

5.6 Findings

My research strategy was to collect data in two cycles. Firstly, I needed to gather information directly from healthcare professionals. The initial cycle of data collection was completed during the month of November 2022 using retrospective information from attendance registers from the *bereavement, grief* and *loss training workshops*, which provided the email addresses of non-attendees. This initial data evidenced that 44.7% did not attend as planned during this month and provided baseline data for non-attendance. All the non-attendees were contacted to complete a survey to gather feedback on why they were unable to attend. The description clearly outlined that the goal was to gather data on non-attendance to inform possible changes and interventions that could support and improve future attendance for healthcare professionals to engage in training opportunities, and that feedback was confidential. The survey questions were kept as minimal as possible. This felt important to highlight to not only encourage compliance but motivate and empower staff to voice their experiences by providing an opportunity to outline the challenges they faced. The survey included free text boxes to encourage this and further support gathering qualitative data.

Six participants (60%) noted work commitments as the reason for their non-attendance on the bereavement, grief and loss workshops, followed jointly by two participants (20%) citing personal reasons and *other* (20%). The two participants who outlined *other* further elaborated that their non-attendance was due to staffing pressures and sickness and had notified me in advance so opted for that response.

When asking healthcare professionals if there was anything that could support their attendance on training in the future, *time* was indicated as a supportive factor, such as study time and appropriate staffing levels to be released to attend.

Reviewing the data from the first survey informed my next cycle of data collection. I used the data and feedback to implement change and see if attendance could be improved. Given the literature review documented management and leadership as an influential factor, it was at this point I decided to test the hypothesis outlined in the research that management buy-in could have a positive impact in promoting learning opportunities, alongside enabling staff to feel valued and supported. I wanted to review and improve the rate of return for my next data cycle, aiming to gather a minimum of 60% response rate in the hope that it would support the validity of my research.

Previously I'd been approached to deliver bereavement, grief and loss training to healthcare staff on a specialist palliative care in-patient unit. This provided me an opportunity to work with the manager to implement and test the following strategies from my data analysis.

1 Managerial support/buy-in – Staff were provided with protected study time to attend, either during work hours or provided time in lieu for attending by the manager.
2 Training delivered face-to-face – I attended their place of work, this was at the request of the manager and staff and I recognised this would be an important factor in supporting attendance and considered Ramani, McMahon and Armstrong's (2019) research in tailoring teaching delivery based on needs of staff.
3 Implemented a QR code to improve feedback survey responses.

I delivered two teaching sessions on the specialist palliative care unit so that all staff had an opportunity to attend. In total, six registered nurses, three healthcare assistants and one student nurse attended. Working directly with the manager of the specialist palliative care unit to support attendance resulted in 83.3% (ten) staff attending, with 16.7% (two) declining due to personal issues. Staff were provided with protected time during working hours or time in lieu for attending on their non-working day. It was evident that management support had a positive impact on the attendance rate. Attendees reported this was a supportive factor, and they felt valued and appreciated by management. The act of providing protected time or being provided time in lieu was an influential incentive to attend the training sessions. One attendee stated 'protected time with absolutely no interference. Thank you. I really appreciated this amazing session'. Another reported training should be provided as an annual refresher, especially given the training was tailored to their area of clinical specialism of palliative care and provided 'one of the best [learning] experiences'.

The second cycle of data was gathered from feedback from attendees in a similar format as the previous Microsoft Teams survey; however, a QR code was introduced. Questions to gather information on attendance and how attendance could be best supported were asked to provide an opportunity to capture if protected time and management support were noted as influential.

If I'd been given more time, had more enthusiasm and discipline to manage the demands of studying on my work/life balance, I would have wanted to complete more data cycles to test the implemented changes in a more structured way. For example, collecting data over several teaching sessions instead of using one session to introduce multiple changes, gathering data over a longer period, working with other managers and teams and having a distinct focus could have afforded more insight and validity. Unfortunately, that wasn't achievable at the time, ironically due to time and workload constraints as I was having to conduct the research within my working day and alongside my role.

5.7 Conclusion

This research, although small in scale, demonstrated that working directly with management can reduce barriers to learning opportunities faced by healthcare professionals and improve attendance. This research provides a strong indication that management support has a positive impact on this cohort. However, further research would be beneficial, particularly on a larger scale across the organisation, which will further validate and build on this research, alongside gaining further insight and understanding into the complexities at play and provide tangible quantitative data.

Recognising the positive role education can play in healthcare, management supporting staff to attend learning opportunities could proactively improve retention, promote well-being, and resilience, alongside gaining further insight into the barriers healthcare staff are facing (Ramani, McMahon and Armstrong, 2019). Patient care will always be prioritised; however, we need to proactively support and recognise the well-being of healthcare professional is vital too. Currently, we have a gap of 4966 full-time equivalent NHS nursing staff in Wales, and Welsh Government is working to improve nursing retention having recognised it's an issue (Church, 2023). The reality is that retention issues are a widespread occurrence across healthcare professionals, and we need to re-look at how we're supporting staff in their roles. The barriers faced may become more extensive, and opportunities to release healthcare staff to attend learning opportunities will become more challenging due to managing staffing levels and patient safety. Investment in adopting a new approach to support staff by providing high-quality educational programmes may provide a solution. Promoting learning opportunities is evidenced to improve not just patient care and outcomes but also staff well-being and retention rates, and this is something important to highlight not only to managers but to those who have influence to implement change on an organisational level (Jiandani et al., 2016). Further supporting this, Walton (2022) highlighted that within the NHS, there's a research gap when it comes to education which is heavily focused on clinical and medical research. More research on the effects education have on healthcare professionals, and in turn on patient experience/outcomes could be of great value. This requires implementing more challenge to change how learning opportunities are valued within an NHS context and requires a systematic approach, as opposed to a localised one as demonstrated in this research project.

Ironically, I undertook this research project wearing many hats, PGCE student, NHS professional/manager/clinical supervisor/educator and single mother. I too experienced the challenges and stress of juggling all the demands and expectations of these roles and feel this limited my ability to be fully present, focused and able to apply myself fully to undertaking the research in a way that I feel it deserved. However, that's not to say it doesn't still have value, I do believe it does; however, it needs further development and analysis.

On an ongoing basis, adopting a research and plan-do-study-act (PDSA) approach facilitates me to drive change. The process of reflecting on the journey provides so much value, learning and data, and when this is applied within my management role within healthcare, this facilitates the main objective, better patient outcomes. Engaging in continued professional development is mandatory for healthcare professionals to maintain registration to practise, as managers we need to be supporting staff in their roles to undertake their responsibilities. Recognising the localised and systemic barriers faced by staff when accessing learning opportunities is vital in effectively offering support that is of value to the individual, team, service, and our patients.

Both my personal and professional hope is that this research or chapter is somewhat thought provoking, or of benefit, at least to minimise the fear of undertaking research and to normalise that if I can do it, anyone can. Although this research won't influence change on a large scale, should one individual find it influential in providing practical ideas to reduce barriers to support and enable staff to access learning opportunities, then that's the silver lining.

References

Church, E. (2023). 'First Time data reveals scale of nursing vacancies in Wales', *Nursing Times*, 14 July. Available at: https://www.nursingtimes.net/news/workforce/first-time-data-reveals-scale-of-nursing-vacancies-in-wales-14-07-2023/#:~:text=The%20new%20experimental%20data%2C%20released,nurses%2C%20midwives%20and%20health%20visitors.&text=This%20put%20the%20vacancy%20rate,the%20quarter%20ending%20December%202022 [Accessed 2 April 2024].

Cohen, L., Manion, L. and Morrison, K. (2018). *Research methods in education*. 8th edn. London: Routledge.

Coventry, T.H., Maslin-Prothero, S.E. and Smith, G. (2015) 'Organizational impact of nurse supply and workload on nurses continuing professional development opportunities: an integrative review', *Journal for Advanced Nursing*, 71(10), pp. 2715–2727.

Holland, P., Tham, T.S., Sheehan, C. and Cooper, B. (2019) 'The impact of perceived workload on nurse satisfaction with work-life balance and intention to leave the occupation', *Applied Nursing Research*, 49, pp. 70–76.

Jiandani, M.P., Bogam, R., Shah, C., Prabhu, S. and Taskande, B. (2016) 'Continous professional development: faculty views on need, impact and barriers', *National Journal of Integrated Research in Medicine*, 7(2), pp. 106–109.

Lumsden, C., Byrne-Davis, L. and Scott, K.M. (2020). 'Blended learning', in Marshall, S. (ed.) *A handbook for teaching and learning in higher education: enhancing academic practice*. 5th edn. London: Routledge, pp. 95–105.

Oldfield, M., Rodwell, J., Curry, L. and Marks, G. (2019) 'A face in a sea of faces: exploring university students' reasons for non-attendance to teaching sessions', *Journal of Further Education*, 43(4), pp. 443–452.

Ramani, S., McMahon, G.T. and Armstrong, E.G. (2019) 'Continuing professional development to foster behavioural change: from principles to practice in health professionals' education', *Medical Teacher*, 41(9), pp. 1045–1052.

Walton, C. (2022) 'Hidden in plain sight', *InTuition*, 49, pp. 32–36.

Chapter 6

Time

The hidden challenge for course leaders for college-based higher education

Clare Sutton

6.1 Introduction

College-based higher education (CBHE) is a sector of higher education (HE) that often goes unseen. The literature on CBHE is limited, and the literature on course leaders (CLs) for CBHE (referred to in this chapter as CLs unless a distinction between CBHE and FE is required) is even more scarce. I worked as a CL for nine years and felt this invisibility. It is with this in mind that turned to research. I wanted to understand the institutional processes that govern the everyday work of CLs and how it often goes unseen and undervalued.

6.2 Research questions

The findings of this research are part of a larger inquiry into the everyday work of CLs. The inquiry did not set out to investigate the issue of time per se; however, it is a theme that arose and in line with my theoretical framework of institutional ethnography (discussed further in Section 6.6), I investigated further. In pursuing this line of inquiry, I asked two questions:

- How do issues relating to time manifest themselves in the everyday work of CLs?
- What are the institutional processes that result in the issues relating to time faced by CLs?

6.3 Positionality

As a CL, I increasingly found myself becoming frustrated with managerial decisions, for example, decisions relating to quality assurances and professional development for the FE sector that did not apply to the HE sector. However, as the HE was part of the College Group, the same policies applied.

It is of note that, in 2022, three years into my part-time PhD research, I resigned from working in the College Group. As a CL, I was at the top of my paygrade with no prospects of moving up the career ladder within CHBE. Leaving was difficult, but I felt that career-wise I had nowhere else to go which

DOI: 10.4324/9781003505389-10

allowed me to remain focused on HE. In 2022, I started a new chapter in my career at the franchising university. I have now also taken on the role of a link tutor at the university, supporting CLs in the partner colleges in writing and delivering the franchised courses.

6.4 Using knowledge

In 1993, the post-incorporated landscape of Further Education (FE) embraced New Public Management (NPM) and its drive for efficiencies, effectiveness and economy. This heralded new contractual arrangements for lecturing staff with increases in workload and contracted hours (Mather, Worrall and Seifert, 2007). Mather, Worrall and Seifert (2007) argued that an aspect of this economic drive took place through two processes: intensification, whereby lecturers workloads increased, and extensification, whereby teaching hours also increased. What were originally denoted as teaching and non-teaching times were redefined by college leaders, with a greater number of hours being allocated to teaching: not having a lecturer in the classroom in front of the students was viewed as inefficient (Mather, Worrall and Seifert, 2007; Turner et al., 2009). This intensification and extensification of teaching came aligned with an increase in student numbers and a reduction in overall numbers of lecturers in the sector leading to fewer lecturers doing more work (Mather, Worrall and Seifert, 2007). Mather, Worrall and Seifert (2007, 2009) further argue that lecturers struggle to keep on top of their workload, with no time to do their job properly and often using their evenings and weekends to complete their workload.

FE colleges often employ CBHE CLs on the same contracts as FE CLs. This means that CBHE CLs have the same number of contracted contact hours and contracts of employment as FE CLs (Tucker, Peddler and Martin, 2020). This is often due to FE colleges not having sufficient HE provision to employ lecturers solely on HE contracts (Keenan, 2020). Furthermore, the fact that in some FE colleges CBHE lecturers are still employed on FE contracts demonstrates a mismatch between HE and FE systems (Turner, McKenzie and Stone, 2009). Feather (2017) found that those with HE responsibilities struggled to complete their everyday work whilst working in an FE environment.

6.5 The existing context

The research was conducted in an FE college group consisting of two FE colleges, a skills training centre, a sixth form college and an alternative provision centre. The College Group is the result of the acquisition of the skills training centre and sixth form, the development of the alternative provision and the merger of a further FE college in 2018, resulting from the government-led, FE area reviews. The five campuses are in the north-east of England. My research was conducted in the two FE colleges that offer CBHE.

Challenges for Course Leaders in College-Based Higher Education 69

The work of a CL is demanding, varied and complex. It is a role that encompasses managing course paperwork, marketing, recruitment, academic duties such as teaching and learning, course development, quality assurance, managing a team, student satisfaction and pastoral work (Cahill et al., 2015; Paterson, 1999; Turner, McKenzie and Stone, 2009). Cahill et al. (2015) refer to a CL as the nominated person for students and course-related issues: someone with many skills for effective course management including the ability to advise, interpret, oversee, inform, counsel, organise and enforce rules. For CLs for CBHE, there is the additional layer of work that results from being part of the HE sector and from the franchising university. For example, this includes differences in quality assurance, differences in the allocation of time for pastoral work (Sutton, 2023) and differences in administrative duties.

6.6 Methodology

Underpinning my research is both the theoretical and methodological framework of Institutional Ethnography. Institutional Ethnography was developed by Dorothy E. Smith (2005). Its aim is not to study people but to map and make visible the ruling relations which organise and coordinate the everyday work of people from a given standpoint (Smith, 2005). Participants were selected on purposive basis: one which identifies and uses individuals with a specific knowledge of professional role (Cohen, Manion and Morrison, 2018; Punch and Oancea, 2014). The standpoint I took up to investigate such ruling relations is that of CLs for CBHE. Taking the standpoint of CLs, I interviewed a number of CLs within the College Group from two different campuses: allowing a wider range of voices to be heard. In addition, in line with an Institutional Ethnographic framework, I interviewed Programme Area Leaders (PALs) who line manage CLs, and those responsible for the strategic operations, members of the Senior Management Team (SMT), in the College Group (see Figure 6.1).

In addition, I analysed institutional texts to look for how the CLs everyday work was organised. Table 6.1 represents the type and sources of data used in this inquiry.

The analysis of the data comes through a process Smith (2005) refers to as mapping. Mapping is used to describe how the analytical process that makes visible the social organisation and ruling relations uncovered in the inquiry. The mapping process involves tracing institutional processes and explaining them, showing how they fit together into sequences of activity which leads back to the everyday work of the adopted standpoint (Smith, 2005). Mapping serves as a guide through the complexities of ruling (DeVault and McCoy, 2002).

Ethical approval and consent for this research were gained from the university where I am studying my PhD. Furthermore, consent was gained from the Chief Executive of the College Group, and individual consent was secured

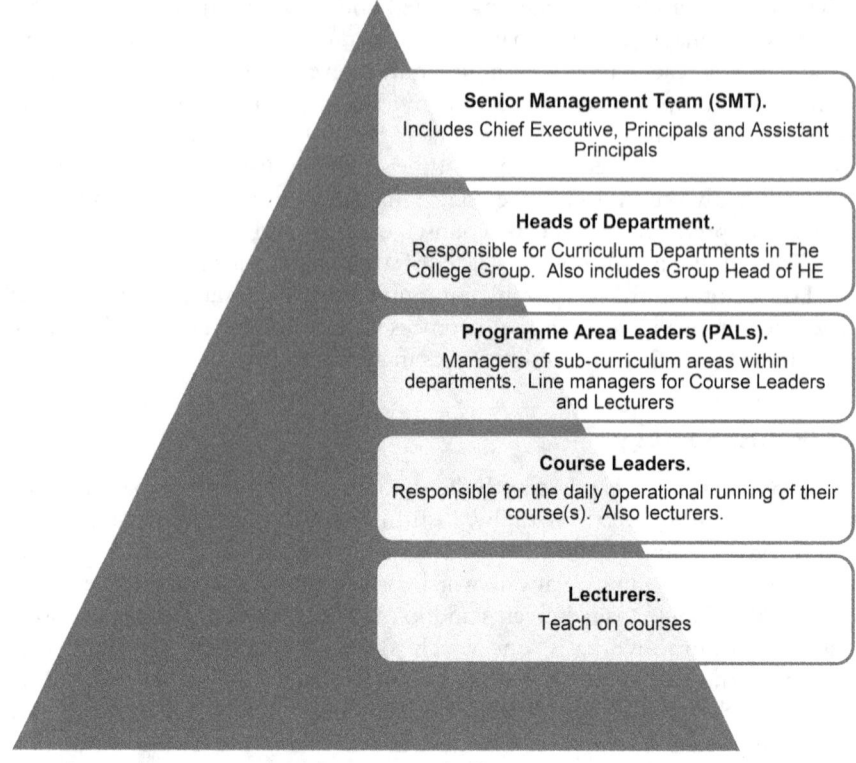

Figure 6.1 Staff structure in the College Group

from each participant taking part. Whilst consent from the awarding university and from individual participants is a requirement of my studies, consent was also sought from the Chief Executive of the College Group. This was important for me as an employee in the College Group as I was seeking to interview his staff and access documents that would not be publicly available.

Table 6.1 Data types and sources used in this research

Data type	Source of data
Interviews (formal and informal)	Course leaders Programme area leaders Senior management team
Texts	Institutional documents • Course leader timetable • Contract of employment
Reflective diary	Researcher

6.7 Findings

Through the interviews with CLs, I found that time is an issue that has been raised on several occasions. The aspect of not having enough time is typified in the quotations below from Vikki and Rebekah.

Vikki talks about the impact that a lack of time to complete her everyday work is having on her work/life balance. She explains that she is working evenings and weekends just to keep on top of her work.

> I don't have enough time to do my job role. I work, probably every night and weekends, just to kind of balance the books really, that stressful. And if I don't do that, then, then I'm swamped.
> (Vikki, CL interview, November 2020)

In her interview, Rebekah talks about not having any time for the CL role and that it is 'extra stuff'. She seems to separate the CL role from the other duties she is responsible for fulfilling. This separation of everyday work comes from having a full-time teaching workload with the additional duties of the CL being added on top of this, something Vikki also discusses.

> You don't get any time for a course leader role, so I think the extra stuff that's expected as course leader is just done in your own time.
> (Rebekah, CL interview, November 2020)

Here, Vikki argued that there is not enough time to balance the two aspects of their everyday work. The arguments from CLs about not being able to complete their everyday work within the bounds of their working week led me to seek out the institutional texts of the *Contract of Employment* (October 2020) and the CL *timetables* (academic year 2021–2022). The *Contract of Employment* states that duties should be able to be performed in a 'normal working week'. Yet, it did not specify what this means. Instead, it has a space for the human resources department to complete upon issuing a course leader their *Contract of Employment*. I was informed by Jason (PAL, informal conversation noted in Reflective Diary, December 2020) that this information is added to reflect the full-time or part-time nature of the employee. For example, a full-time CL will have 37.5 hours added into their contract. Yet, this does not reflect the number of teaching hours that are expected of the CL. This led to further questions being asked of PALs, Sam and Jason (PAL interviews, June 2021 and July 2021, respectively). In their interviews, both confirmed that the number of teaching hours for all full-time teaching staff, including CLs, is 864 hours per academic year.

However, there were inconsistencies that were highlighted when looking at the number of teaching hours on CLs *timetables*. I noted that the number of teaching hours allocated to full-time CLs ranges between around 650 hours (Charlotte) to over 900 hours (Vikki). The CL timetabled for 650 hours took part in this research. In her interview, she did not discuss any further responsibilities in her everyday work. There was one part-time course leader, Eric on a 0.5 contract, allocated 529 teaching hours. Whilst the number of full-time teaching hours should work out at 24 hours per week, if taking the annual hours of 864 over the duration of an FE course at 36 weeks, Vikki and Eric are not alone in having more teaching hours.

Returning to the *Contracts of Employment* for CLs for CBHE, I found that these are the same as those for FE CLs (Harwood and Harwood, 2004; Turner, McKenzie and Stone, 2009). Yet, FE contracts lack the time needed for those with HE responsibilities to meet the demands of their role (Turner, McKenzie and Stone, 2009). These additional demands include writing curriculums for the university, additional moderation meetings, scholarly activity and liaising with both the partner university and other partner colleges. It is argued that teaching CBHE 24 hours per week or more leaves little time for anything else (Feather, 2017; Harwood and Harwood, 2004). My data showed that CLs found it difficult to meet the demands of their everyday work within the bounds of a 'normal working week'. This was due to the high teaching workload of at least 24 hours being allocated to CL. The difficulties stem from the *Contracts of Employment and Timetables* not taking account of the additional workload faced by CL for CBHE (Feather, 2017; Turner, McKenzie and Stone, 2009).

As in my interviews with Rebekah and Vikki, Charlotte draws attention to the issue of extra workload. In particular, she focused on a lack of understanding of the additional duties CLs have over lecturers and CLs for FE courses in the College Group.

> I'm not sure the college really understands that when you're a Course leader for at the difference that that extra workload is dealing with, you know, the partnership as well. So, I don't think that's always appreciated.
> (Charlotte, CL interview, October 2020)

In the College Group, HE courses are delivered via a franchise arrangement with Waterside University. A part of the everyday work of the CLs involves liaising with other colleges also in the franchise partnership and the link tutors at Waterside University to ensure that all of the academic and assessment processes are completed in line with the *Quality Framework* at Waterside University. However, from speaking with Christina and Joe, members of the SMT, I would argue that the additional work of the CLs is understood.

Christina (SMT) highlighted this additional work for the CL; she described it as an extra layer of work. The additional layer of work adds to the workload of the CL and thus impacts the time they have to complete their everyday work.

> There are two at least two additional layers to the course leader role, for HE provision than for FE provision. It's more complex
> (Christina, SMT interview, Oct 2021)

Joe (SMT) highlighted that CLs have additional duties due to the university partnership's requirements.

> And then there's also the additional things that were required from the university so I know Course leaders attend meetings with the university and, you know…and then also the additional duties to fulfil their course leader role so I think time could potentially be at the forefront…
>
> (Joe, SMT interview, June 2021)

Given that the additional work of the CLs is understood by members of the SMT, I questioned why it is not taken into consideration in the teaching workload of the CLs. It seems the tensions relating to completing their everyday work by CLs come from the FE model in which the HE is being delivered. A model that is grounded in NPM and efficiency, economy and effectiveness where non-teaching work is often seen as 'covert duties' and does not have time allocated for it (Randle and Brady, 1997; Sutton, 2023).

> I think it is teaching HE in an FE provision, because we are actually teaching it under FE guidelines, erm, teaching hours, delivery modes and things like that. I think it is no additional time for HE, so doing academic research…I think it has also become quite evident this year with re-writing the programmes as well
>
> (Elizabeth, CL interview, October 2020)

Elizabeth is highlighting that the lack of time to be able to engage in scholarly activity and research to support the curriculum development and teaching is due to the HE being college-based. She argues that the issues arise from the HE and FE models not aligning (Turner, McKenzie and Stone, 2009).

The Higher Education Funding Council for England (HEFCE, 2009) stated that there should be a reduction in teaching hours for those teaching CBHE. Prior to 2014, this was something the CLs for HE in the College Group experienced. In her interview, Elizabeth further discussed that time used to be allocated for additional duties relating to being a course leader.

> You got 120 hours a year course leader time which is about half a day per week you were given for course leadership roles and responsibilities and that was really helpful no, that got stopped now… When I first started teaching HE we were given 20 minutes… or something
>
> (Elizabeth, CL Interview, October 2020)

The 20 minutes Elizabeth was discussing was the time allowed for planning, preparation and marking for HE. This was an allowance for all lecturers teaching higher education, and it was at the rate of 20 minutes remission from the annual teaching hours for each hour the lecturer/CL taught HE. Both the CL time and this additional remission ceased in 2014. Although this remission ceased prior to my data collection, as it had been raised in an interview, I asked Simon (SMT) about this in an informal interview (Reflective Diary, December 2020). He explained that it was the previous Head of Finance who removed this allocation as it was not classed as an efficient use of time, when the time could be spent in the classroom with learners. Therefore, whilst the time allocation for being a course leader was taken away and replaced with teaching hours, the work for the CL was not reduced, simply squeezed into their non-contact time and impacting their work/life balance.

6.8 Conclusions

My research highlighted that *Contracts of Employment* did not differentiate between CLs for HE and FE (Harwood and Harwood, 2004; Turner, McKenzie and Stone, 2009). Yet, this is something that is not unusual for CBHE CLs due to colleges having insufficient HE provision to allow for staff to be on separate contracts (Keenan, 2020). Yet, this one-size-fits-all approach has an impact on the everyday work of the CLs for CBHE. CLs struggle to complete their everyday work within the bounds of a typical working week (Tucker, Peddler and Martin, 2020; Feather, 2017). A particularly pertinent point was, unlike other research that found that the additional workload was not acknowledged (Tucker, Peddler and Martin, 2020), it was clear that members of the SMT were aware of these additional duties. However, this awareness did not translate into additional time for these duties: duties such as partnership work with the franchising university, scholarly activity and writing curriculum materials (Lea and Simmons, 2012). It is clear that there is a mismatch between FE and HE everyday work, with the models of FE and HE not aligning, forcing many CLs to work outside of their typical working week and impacting their work/life balance (Feather, 2017; Harwood and Harwood, 2004; Tucker, Peddler and Martin, 2020; Turner, McKenzie and Stone, 2009). My research led me to conclude that the NPM that pervades FE colleges has resulted in the issues with time faced by CLs.

The prevalence in NPM was no more so evident in the decisions underpinning the workload of the CLs than in the removal of scholarly activity time for those teaching on HE courses. The removal of this time due to it being an inefficient use of time echoes the discourse of NPM and its focus on efficiency, economy and effectiveness (Randle and Brady, 1997). In 2020, at the time I started my data collection, there was no sign of a reduction in hours as proposed by HEFCE (2009) nor the remission for being a course leader or teaching HE. Instead, the College group was reflecting the FE sector more broadly with CBHE CLs being employed on FE contracts and having over

800 hours of annual teaching (Creasy, 2013). The issues experienced by the CLs surrounding time arise from college management and policies which try to shoehorn college-based higher education into existing FE contracts and working conditions (Tucker, Peddler and Martin, 2020).

Having shared the findings of my research with peers from the CBHE sector, it is clear that the College Group is not alone in the way it manages CLs for CBHE. My hope is that we, as practitioners, are able to continue to find the time and motivation to conduct research into our often forgotten about sector. It is through research that we can illuminate the issues faced by CLs for CBHE and hopefully start to make a difference in the sector.

References

Cahill, J., Bowyer, J., Rendell, C., Hammond, A. and Korek, S. (2015) 'An exploration of how programme leaders in higher education can be prepared and supported to discharge their roles and responsibilities effectively', *Educational Research*, 57(3), pp. 272–286.

Cohen, L., Manion, L. and Morrison, K. (2018) *Research methods in education*. 8th edn. London: Routledge

Creasy, R. (2013) 'HE lite: exploring the problematic position of HE in FECs', *Journal of Further and Higher Education*, 37(1), pp. 38–53.

DeVault, M.L. and McCoy, L. (2002) 'Institutional ethnography: using interviews to investigate ruling relations', in Jaber, G. and James, H. (eds) *Handbook of interview research*. Thousand Oaks, CA: Sage Publications, pp. 751–776.

Feather, D. (2017) 'Time! What's that? You're joking, I don't have any!', *Journal of Further and Higher Education*, 41(5), pp. 706–716.

Harwood, D. and Harwood, J. (2004) 'Higher education in further education: delivering higher education in a further education context – a study of five South West colleges', *Journal of Further and Higher Education*, 28(2), pp. 153–164.

HEFCE. (2009) *Supporting higher education in further education colleges: policy, practice and prospects*. Bristol: HEFCE.

Keenan, J. (2020) '*The CBHE lecturer and student*', in Kadi-Hanifi, K. and Keenan, J. (eds.) *College based higher education and its identities history, pedagogy and purpose within the sector*. Cham: Palgrave McMillan, pp. 23–42.

Lea, J. and Simmons, J. (2012) 'Higher education in further education: capturing and promoting HEness', *Research in Post-Compulsory Education*, 17(2), pp. 179–193.

Mather, K., Worrall, L. and Seifert, R. (2007) 'Reforming further education: the changing labour process for college lecturers', *Personnel Review*, 36(1), pp. 109–127.

Mather, K., Worrall, L. and Seifert, R. (2009) 'The changing locus of workplace control in the English further education sector', *Employee Relations*, 31(2), pp. 139–157.

Paterson, H. (1999) 'The changing role of the course leader within a higher education/further education context', *Research in Post Compulsory Education*, 4(1), pp. 97–116.

Punch, K.F. and Oancea, A. (2014) *Introduction to research methods in education*. 2nd edn. London: Sage Publications Ltd.

Randle, K. and Brady, N. (1997) 'Further education and new managerialism', *Journal of Further and Higher Education*, 21(2), pp. 229–239.

Smith, D.E. (2005) *Institutional ethnography a sociology for people*. Oxford: Alta Mira Press.

Sutton, C. (2023) 'An institutional ethnographic investigation into the pastoral work of course leaders for college-based higher education', *Research in Post Compulsory Education*, 28(4), pp. 1–17.

Tucker, C., Peddler, S. and Martin, G. (2020) '*The CBHE lecturer experience*', in Kadi-Hanifi, K. and Keenan, J. (eds.) *College based higher education and its identities history, pedagogy and purpose within the sector*. Cham: Palgrave McMillan, pp. 89–102.

Turner, R., McKenzie, L.M., McDermott, A.P. and Stone, M. (2009) 'Emerging HE cultures: perspectives from CETL award holders in a partner college network', *Journal of Further and Higher Education*, 33(3), pp. 255–263.

Turner, R., McKenzie, L. and Stone, M. (2009) "Square peg - round Hole': the emerging professional identities of HE in FE lecturers working in a partner college network in South-West England', *Research in Post Compulsory Education*, 14(4), pp. 355–368.

Chapter 7

Making learning diaries meaningful for learners in the community

Chloë Hynes

7.1 Research questions and or aims and objectives

At the time of this research, I was teaching beginner ESOL (English for Speakers of Other Languages) courses for the adult and community learning service for my local council. Our Self Assessment Report (SAR) had identified that our service needed to improve on learner feedback, and after discussions with colleagues, we agreed that my focus would be on investigating and improving the organisation's learning diary which all learners had to complete. ESOL learners had difficulties in using this compulsory diary, and I wanted to investigate how the format of the diary, and our teaching approach, could be reimagined so that it nurtured the skill of individual reflection, charted a learner's journey through the course and provided meaningful feedback for learners and teachers.

7.2 Positionality

During the early years as a newly qualified teacher, I had been accepted to research this issue as part of the Practitioner Led Action Research (PLAR) programme, and received support from East Midlands Centre for Excellence in Teacher Training (emCETT) which was funded by the Education and Training Foundation (ETF). I also opted to complete a Level 5 module in Action Research as part of this project as I was motivated to improve my practice.

The organisation I worked for was the adult and community learning (ACL) service for my local council. Most of our courses were non-accredited and in order to ensure they were just as rigorous as accredited courses we would undertake a RARPA (Recognising and Recording Progress and Achievement) process. For each learner, we had a 10-page document in shades of teal called the PLR (Personal Learning Record). This document was mass printed and given to every teacher from family learning to photography and beginners Spanish to ESOL. Whilst a pre-printed document ensured consistency and convenience across the service, it was not easily adaptable to individual learner needs and created a sense of apathy amongst tutors and learners alike.

My previous experience of utilising the PLR was challenging as students struggled to find it engaging and saw it as a tick box activity. Some commented on its negative connotations as they felt it reminded them of their job centre journal (many of our learners were unemployed and some were referred to the service by their job advisors) or other 'official forms'. The ESOL learners in particular found it incredibly difficult to write developmental reflections in the non-native language they were beginning to learn. The project was about making written feedback 'do-able', and I didn't think the PLR was 'do-able' for teachers or learners. I felt it was restrictive and not conducive to meaningful interaction, so I wanted to test that and see if an alternative could be developed that nurtured, rather than spoiled teachers' relationships with learners. As it was a document that many of my colleagues didn't like, I thought it was important to use the opportunity to be pro-active and discover whether it could be utilised in a more productive way.

7.3 Using knowledge

The Education Endowment Foundation (EEF) developed useful guidance (Collin and Quigley, 2021), which explored ways to give effective feedback to learners and encourage them to reflect and evaluate their learning autonomously. Whilst this report was situated for primary and secondary audiences, the theoretical underpinnings of metacognition and ways in which we learn are a good starting point for those of us working in FE, particularly when supporting our learners to 'learn how to learn'.

Phil Race's *Making Learning Happen* (2010) was a pivotal read for me around the time I conducted the research. Here, he detailed multiple approaches to feedback and the importance of closing the loop providing evidence of learner 'reflections as part of an ongoing process of becoming increasingly conscious of how they learn' (Race, 2010, p. 121). He also suggested giving feedback to learners after they have completed a self-assessment so the tutor feedback would be 'much more focused on learners' real needs than just giving feedback without knowing what learners themselves already thought about their own strengths and weaknesses...' (Race, 2010, p. 110). This focus on making feedback relevant was particularly important to me as I was keen to ensure the new PLR would be purposeful.

Working for ACL, teaching mainly non-accredited courses meant needing to have a firm grasp of RARPA (Figure 7.1) and its processes. The original PLR was designed to make this process consistent across the service and encouraged different levels of target setting and tutor feedback on a session-by-session basis. In 2017, the Learning and Work Institute (LWI) issued a report about the 'expanding role of RARPA'. The team conducted research in effective practice within the sector and developed an accompanying case studies booklet. The report (LWI, 2017, p. 5) encourages providers to expand the use of Individual Learning Plans (ILPs) beyond a one-size-fits-all

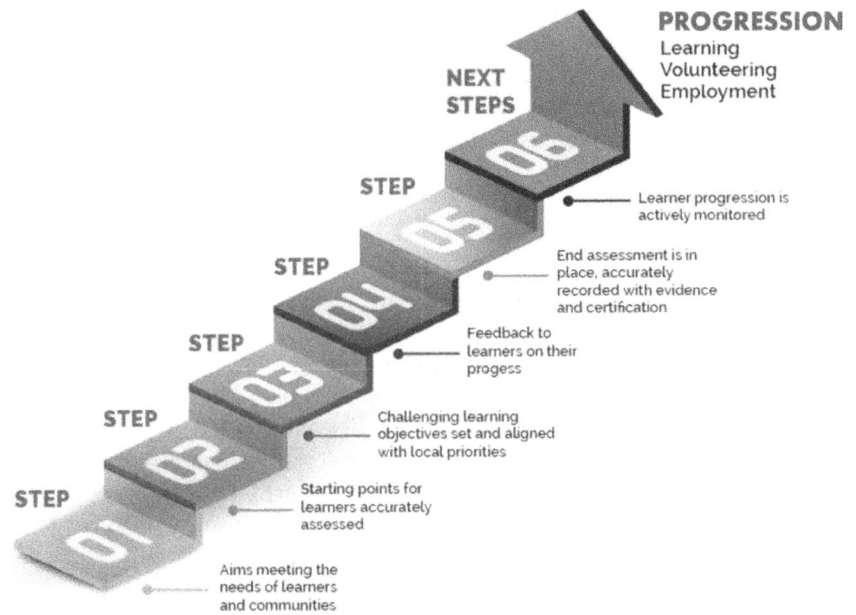

Figure 7.1 The five-step RARPA process including a final sixth step as proposed by LWI (LWI, 2017, p. 7)

document because 'being non-prescriptive allows the provider to determine which approach works best for them and their learners in local circumstances'. Most importantly, the report reminds us that the fundamental principle of the RARPA process is to 'place the learner at the centre of the learning process'.

An integral part of ILPs is goal setting. SMART targets are often recommended, yet they are a controversial subject within FE, not least because they were not developed for our sector in the first place. As ESOL Specialist Sam Shepherd said in his journal article titled 'It's Best Practice': SMART targets – evidence or assertion? (2017), 'SMART targets do not reflect how learners learn'. He goes on to explain this is because such formulaic targets 'suggest we are dealing with a direct, predictable linear process and that once this has been achieved, said language is now "known"'. For ESOL learners specifically, we have further considerations in that ILPs are generally written in English which is the target language itself; thus, the learner has to reflect on, and set goals for, their learning in the language they are trying to acquire (Sutter, 2009, p. 208). As such, the PLR provided an extra challenge for my learners not least because they needed to utilise and learn a metalanguage used in reflection, which is a skill in its own right. However, there has been practitioner research done in the sector which explores ways in which to develop meaningful targets such as the OTLA (Outstanding Teaching, Learning and

Assessment) action research project 'Supporting learner ownership and the formulation of authentic goals' carried out by ESOL and English practitioners at East London Advanced Technology Training (ELATT, 2022) and ways in which to make evaluation accessible using 'Emojis in ESOL and English' conducted by practitioners at Kendal College and South Lakes Community Learning (ETF, 2021).

7.4 The existing context

The context this research was carried out in was an adult community and family learning provider in the north of England. A provision held under the local council to fulfil the councils' aims of improving the lives of disadvantaged people within the locale. The curriculum area under which the project team worked was Skills for Life (maths, English and ESOL). The aim of these courses was to reduce isolation and encourage learners to progress onto further learning opportunities to improve their English. The cohorts I worked with on this project were mostly unemployed, and some students were neurodivergent with specific learning differences and needs.

After the initial research period, the research continued in a range of ESOL classes from those new to ESOL (beginners) to Entry Level 2. Courses were five weeks and 10 weeks long. All one two-hour sessions a week. This was often a challenging but necessary way in which to work within ACL as teachers must decipher exactly what learners need over the coming weeks and how to help them, negotiate a developmental ILP and facilitate it in an incredibly short amount of time. This often fed into one of the complaints from teachers about the PLR; that this document took up too much teaching and learning time. Likewise, students commented that it was a 'waste of time' with 'too many forms', and it felt like 'I was back at school'.

7.5 Methodology

The approach I used was practitioner-led research, and I was heavily inspired by the cyclical nature of action research recommended by McNiff (2017) which proposes making small changes in your practice, reflecting on the impact, exploring further changes and amendments, reflecting again and so on. Simply put, action research involves 'real people who are evaluating their practice with a view to improving it' (McNiff, 2017, p. 34). I find this approach conducive to my professional teaching practice because I'm a highly reflective teacher who is constantly seeking to improve teaching, learning and (all forms of) assessment for her learners. Beyond this, action research is a values-based practice which allows the practitioner to take what is personally and professionally important to them and study it. Stenhouse (1975, p. 143), one of the original supporters of the methodology in the UK, proposes that 'it is not enough that teachers' work should be studied: they need to study it themselves'. When I was a new teacher, this quote particularly resonated with me because there were elements of pedagogical practice that didn't sit well with my burgeoning values as a teacher (e.g. SMART targets, one size fits all documents), but I didn't feel I had the power to argue against it. I now understand this is an example of epistemic injustice; a silencing and exclusion of ideas causing professionals to feel as though they cannot argue against mainstream pedagogical ideas. Most recently, Glen et al. describe action research enabling teachers' agency providing them with '...a connection between doing educational research in one's practice and the sense of taking control of, and doing something about, one aspect of your practice' (2023, p. 25). This was certainly true for me.

Doing research on my own teaching practice encouraged me to work collaboratively on a project with my peers on a common theme with individual lines of enquiry making knowledge claims collaboratively. It also gave me the opportunity to research in practice with, and alongside, my class by developing and redeveloping drafts of the learning diary (Figure 7.2); co-creating aspects of it with my learners, discovering which sections were most meaningful to them and most importantly; why. The project was 'triangulated' (ETF, 2021, p. 14) as I was supported to understand the 'complex nature of the learner's world' through reflections and opinions of my peers, learners and of course myself. A unique aspect of action research is how it is 'conducted *with* others rather than *on* others...grounded in values of social justice and equity' (Glenn, Sullivan and Roche, 2023, p. 24). From my experience on this project, learners were proud to be part of something where they could affect change in the organisation and have a profound impact on future learners.

7.6 Findings

Through the various iterations of the learning diaries I produced, I found that students were put off by too much text. However, their engagement increased when emojis and graphics were used instead. For short courses, learners did not want to spend a lot of their time translating and completing forms as it wasn't a worthwhile activity for them. In the initial investigation, all of the learners preferred the new form (Figure 7.2) and found it 'engaging' and 'a fun way to keep a record' of the work they had done. It helped them to visually see the distance they had travelled.

Learners appreciated the brief recorded written feedback as a reference tool, and all learners successfully reflected using visuals such as thermometers, arrows and emojis. However, only 60% of students reflected in written English. I found that ESOL and literacy learners, in particular, struggled with the skill of reflection (made all the more challenging in their target language) and

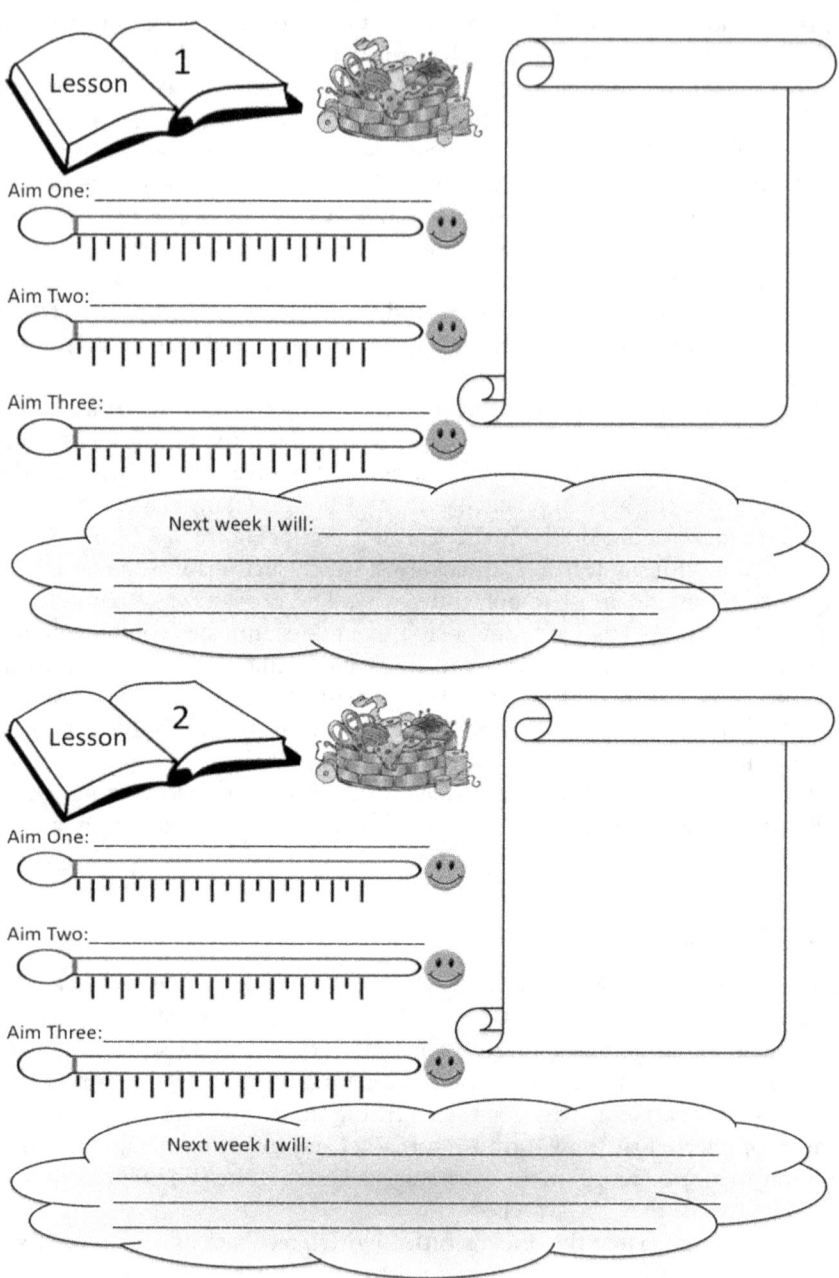

Figure 7.2 Newly designed lesson reflection pages

constructing SMART targets. As such, I began to encourage learners to write using L1 (first, native or other languages), so language was not a barrier in their reflection. Whilst this led to an increase in engagement with the written sections, the approach was criticised by the standardisation team as they had concerns that I would not know what my learners had written. As I didn't think, it was pivotal that I needed to be able to read their personal written reflections if they had provided a visual representation elsewhere, this led me to reflect on who the real audience of the learning diary (and the whole RARPA process) was.

7.6.1 Continuing the Learning

Following this intervention, I was encouraged to explore ways in which I could 'facilitate a learner's involvement with, reflection on and crucially, ownership of the act or process of learning' (Sutter, 2009, p. 208). This included personal word lists, gluing in images/work and mini certificates of achievement. I believe that the RARPA process is most effective when it is most authentic to the learners needs, involving them meaningfully every step of the way. Ultimately, the focus must be on the personal reflection of their learning journey rather than their ability to use and write in English.

After the initial PLAR project had finished, I was tasked with continuing my (re)development of the PLR, and this is where the impact of the project was made visible. This redevelopment was a personal continuation of the research project away from the original project group (whilst still utilising their collaboration and support at specific points). Additionally, after this project had ended, practitioners were given permission to amend and adapt the PLR which demonstrated the high levels of trust managers had in their teachers to do so. This was the start of my interest in and passion for action research as I had experienced first-hand through my small project how it can usher in culture change within an organisation.

7.7 Conclusions

- For those seeking to use RARPA processes for unaccredited courses (or make an effective record of a learner journey in other courses), utilise something which is both **adaptable and editable** in a way that makes it work for the teachers, the subject and the learners themselves.
- Make the diary a **routine and integral part of the lesson,** not just an add on. For example, I had red, green, and orange pens in a particular pencil case for colouring their reflection arrows at different points during the session and course (Figure 7.3). After making it a staple part of our lesson routine, my learners were autonomously completing this task as they arrived and before leaving without me having to ask them. I also had symbols for the core ESOL skills on the board (Figures 7.4 and 7.5) to share what

Figure 7.3 Initial reflection page from the learner diary for beginners ESOL

skills we were focusing on that day as a way to grade the language of the learning objectives. Learners recognized these as the aims (rather than long complex English sentences).
- Teachers should be **empowered** (and most importantly: **trusted**) to make these changes in a way that remains sufficient for RARPA evidence. This could be done in collaboration with peers (and where possible, cohorts) to share ideas.
- An **action research** approach was the appropriate strategy for this project as it allowed me to keep building on and reflecting on the document until its final iteration (version 9 with add-on sheets for specific learners or cohorts).
- Design **pick and mix style pages** and allow the addition of stapled/glued in excerpts dependent on need and relevance to the subject.

Making Learning Diaries Meaningful for Learners in the Community 85

This is my diary.

Username: _____

Password: _____

edmodo

A a B b C c D d E e F f G g
H h I i J j K k L l M m N n
O o P p Q q R r S s T t
U u V v W w X x Y y Z z

Date	I learned:	✓	My teacher says:
	reading		
	writing		
	speaking		
	listening		
	grammar		
	maths		

new words:

Figure 7.4 Session reflection page from the learner diary for beginners ESOL

- Nurture **learner ownership** of the diary and encourage them to not only record their learning journey but celebrate it. This will help to make it more meaningful to the learner and their lives.
- Use an **online diary** if more appropriate for your cohort. Use a freemium EdTech platform such as Padlet or Wakelet which would allow for multimodal and multisensory responses whilst nurturing learner's digital literacies. Here is an example template for a learning diary which you are welcome to copy and reuse. It has been created using Wakelet which has an embedded immersive reader and translator for accessibility: bit.ly/Wakelet_ILP.
- Consider language and format of the document throughout to make it **accessible, user-friendly and purposeful** (and not reminiscent of a job centre form or booklet).

Figure 7.5 Photo of my interactive core skills board

This was my first action research project, and it lay the foundations for a considered approach to my teaching practice where I was increasingly more aware of my personal values, which were made clear from the research I chose to undertake. From this project onwards, I found that if I encountered a problem or a tough challenge, or perhaps there was something I didn't like or agree with, an action research project allowed me to test things out, trial them and assess the impact working alongside the learners. It is an approach that I find empowering as a teaching professional but when working alongside learners it can be empowering for them too as they know they are working to improve their own class community and the work may have ripples beyond their classroom.

References

Collin, J. and Quigley, A. (2021) *Teacher feedback to improve pupil learning: guidance report* [Online]. London: EEF. Available at: https://educationendowmentfoundation.org.uk/education-evidence/guidance-reports/feedback/?gad_source=1&gclid=CjwKCAjwz42xBhB9EiwA48pT7wyam5Z1Oi3IXdD0cMmH8Tv0WarECpog2rR5moJS2d4dH1jEuLC8UxoCQmQQAvD_BwE [Accessed: 21 May 2024].

ELATT. (2022) *Supporting learner ownership and the formulation of authentic goals* [Online]. London: ETF. Available at: https://ccpathways.co.uk/practitioner-research/otla8/13c/ [Accessed: 21 May 2024].

ETF. (2021) *Doing action research – a guide for post-16 practitioners*. London: ETF.

Glenn, M., Sullivan, B. and Roche, M., et al. (2023) *Action research for the classroom*. Oxon: Routledge.

Kendal College and South Lakes Community Learning. (2021) *Emojis in English and ESOL* [Online]. London: ETF. Available at: https://ccpathways.co.uk/practitioner-research/otla-7/cluster-1/7-1/ [Accessed: 21 May 2024].

LWI. (2017) *Quality assuring non-regulated provision: the expanding role of RARPA*. Leicester: National Learning and Work Institute.

McNiff, J. (2017) *Action research for professional development*. Dorset: September Books.

Race, P. (2010) *Making learning happen*. 2nd edn. London: Sage.

Shepherd, S. (2017) 'It's Best Practice': SMART targets – evidence or assertion?', *Language Issues*, 27(2), pp. 38–47.

Stenhouse, L. (1975) *An introduction to curriculum research and development*. London: Heinemann.

Sutter, J. (2009) 'Planning and assessment: reflection, evaluation and the learning cycle', in Paton, A. and Wilkins, M. (eds.) *Teaching adult ESOL*. England: Open University Press, pp. 188–210.

Part III

Models for practitioner research in FE

Chapter 8

Coleg Sir Gar Coleg Ceredigion

The evolution of our Culture of Curiosity

Bryony Evett Hackfort

8.1 Opening

A meaningful, self-sustaining, practitioner-led action research culture can't happen overnight. It can't happen without transparency, trust and open minded leadership. It can't happen without the willingness and commitment to sincerely put the teacher's voice first. An embedded action research culture has to be rooted in an evolutionary language of personal and professional development that places the individual and their self-reflected needs at its core.

In 2015, our then Director of Teaching, Learning and now Vice Principal for Curriculum and Quality recognised the urgent and essential need to design a bespoke framework of professional learning. It was essential to bring the teacher's voice into the professional learning process which was achieved through the introduction of a yearly self-evaluation that sat as the foundation of our new professional learning framework 'The Pathways of Excellence' (Daniels, 2019).

> The digital self-evaluation was designed internally using published educational research into effective evidenced based Teaching and Learning competencies. Teachers self-assess fifty-four competencies grading themselves on a scale of 1–4 which link to the four Excellence Pathways (Developing, Continuing, Advancing and Extended). This provides teachers with a digital portrait of their perceived strengths and areas for development and initiates discussion regarding training and development as part of the appraisal process with their line manager. The foundation of the Pathways of Excellence is inclusivity and personalisation so there is a place for every teacher in the organisation on the Pathway continuum. The Pathway accommodates the individual's needs, no matter where the individual finds themselves.
>
> (Daniels, 2019)

This self-evaluation and the outcomes served as a catalyst for professional dialogue with line managers, peers and the central teaching and learning team in order to create tailored opportunities for focused improvement bespoke to each practitioner. The self-evaluation competencies have evolved with time as the teaching and learning landscape transforms, but always at its heart is the teacher, their strengths, their areas for improvement and personalised development opportunities.

The self-evaluation process formed the foundation of our award winning Pathways of Excellence (Daniels, 2019) that allowed us to embark on the next evolutionary stage of our approach to professional learning with the launch of our Culture of Curiosity in 2018.

We felt strongly that the next evolutionary stage of our Pathways of Excellence lies within practitioner-led action research. We wanted a mechanism of professional learning that was rooted in an evidence-based process, empowered curiosity and led to professional collaboration, dialogue and sharing. This process also allowed new and forward-thinking teaching and learning methodologies to be tried, tested and ultimately scaled up to benefit our wider college community. At its heart, a well-designed and leadership supported-action research programme empowers educators to be agents of change in their own classrooms and colleges, driving continuous improvement and innovation in teaching and learning processes.

8.2 Research questions and or aims and objectives

We had one clear aim.

To establish a genuine, teacher led, action research culture in a Further Education (FE) institution.

A classic FE attitude of 'go big or go home'.

It was quickly clear from the outset that the scale of this project was substantial, and it was key to ensure that we did not rush this process. Honestly, at the beginning, it was difficult to define our aim and even more so how we were going to get there. Education moves fast, workload is immense, time is tight and funds are scarce. It was clear that we could roll out an action research initiative that could find natural momentum in year 1, perhaps may have some interest in year 2 but would be a distant memory by year 3.

We knew that we wanted more than this.

We wanted something that would genuinely change the way in which we worked and had purpose. In order to do this, we knew that ultimately this culture needed to positively impact the learners and enhance their own learning experience.

As educators, we always talk about wanting our learners to be interested in their own learning, to be curious and to see value in lifelong learning. We want our learners to care. We want our learners to see that they have it within them to solve problems and make a difference. How do we 'teach' them this? We don't. We model it. We practice what we preach. We don't ask anything of them that we wouldn't do ourselves.

From this point, we became clear about the 'Why' of what we were trying to achieve and could set our path. This allowed us to create a more meaningful aim that was actionable and could be communicated to our college community. Our Culture of Curiosity was the framework that would give our lecturers the space to explore and experiment whilst giving the college a quality-assured process to give peace of mind.

Now that we had a clear purpose, we could redefine our aim.

Our newly defined aim was to create an open and transparent culture in which practitioners feel safe to explore and experiment with action research within a nurturing and skills-focused framework.

Our objectives were to:

1 Provide an inclusive action research programme to all staff regardless of research experience, level of teaching and subject area.
2 Empower our staff, encouraging them to recognise their own potential, challenge assumptions and develop faith in their voice and expertise.
3 Share their practice both internally and on a regional and national platform.

From the outset, it was clear that for this to work, our Senior Leadership team would need to play an active role. A genuine, invested consideration of the findings and recommendations that the staff identified. A genuine culture of listening. Listening that leads to meaningful action. For staff to invest their time, it was key that the outcomes were valued and not just a pretty end product to prove engagement. In order to achieve this, the notion of curiosity needed to be strategically embedded into the college values and behaviours.

Our commitment to research is reflected from our high-level college strategic plan through to our operational plan specifically within Teaching and Learning. The flow chart below extracts the key statements from each document that show how curiosity is embedded at every level so that it is owned by us all.

8.2.1 College-wide vision

'to encourage curiosity and creativity in teaching and learning'

↓

8.2.2 College-wide strategic objective: outstanding teaching and learning (1 of 4)

'be renowned for exceptional standards, research and innovation in teaching and learning'

↓

8.2.3 Teaching and learning vision

Our vision is of becoming a recognised centre for post-compulsory educational research in Wales, through developing an inspiring and innovative teaching and learning culture, underpinned by staff research. We are striving to encourage all staff regardless of experience, level of teaching and subject area to undertake close to practice research in order to enhance the teaching and learning experience college wide.

↓

8.2.4 Teaching and learning objectives

'Increase capacity, reach and engagement with the Action Research pathway across every faculty'

'Work with Faculty Management teams to explore the use of the research findings to enhance the curriculum and learner experience'

'Develop a technique-focused guest speaker programme to develop the quality and standard of the action research projects'

8.3 Positionality

Being able to articulate the purpose of this work was fundamental and in the early days this was extremely difficult. I frequently felt misunderstood when trying to seek advice and establish collaborative working with other sectors. FE sat outside of long established and funded cross-sector working relationships where there was always a seemingly 'parent and child' set up.

The notion of research lives in 'academia'. Rightly or wrongly, it always has. This has created barriers and places a series of assumptions as to the level of value placed on an individual's thinking based on role, qualifications and status. I wanted parity for our staff. I did not want to settle for a framework that did not recognise the expertise of the FE practitioner or made their value any less than other sectors. However, trying to explain this was just hard. I didn't have the language to express what we wanted to achieve. This changed once I looked UK wide for support and inspiration, and I was introduced to the thinking of Sam Jones through Solihull College & University Centre's FE Researchmeet. Sam Jones spoke a language that immediately stood out and made sense. Sam discussed the idea of action research meaningfully 'Feeding the Tree' (Jones, 2020) so that the practitioner work 'fed' the organisation and its operation rather than simply 'decorate' and be presented to inspectors and VIPs. As Jones states in her 2020 TES article, 'we need to use the research to develop and nourish our sector' and this sentiment struck a deep chord with what we were trying but could not find a way to say. This online event and presentation was pivotal in giving us a clear and articulate language that allowed us to be concise about what we wanted to achieve and the values driving our work. Five years on, we continue to assess all of our decisions in relation to professional learning through action research by asking ourselves whether new ideas genuinely 'Feed the tree' (Jones, 2020) or are simply decorative.

Hearing Sam speak gave us the confidence to challenge the longstanding assumptions that 'we' have about research. Who can do it? Who should do it? What does it look like? Who should learn from it? How should it be presented? We wanted to remove the exclusivity and hierarchy of 'Research' and open it up to all. In the early days, suggestions were made not to refer to our work as research and maybe what we were doing were projects. Immediately, the work was being labelled as lesser. We stood firm.

For us, parity of esteem, equality and inclusivity was paramount so staff from across the whole organisation knew that their voice and thinking mattered. Regardless of whether you had a full-time contract or not, regardless of how long you had been with us, regardless of whether you had five degrees or none… you have a place on our programme if you are curious. You don't have to be curious about everything, but be curious about something. You can make a difference, what do you want to change? We are currently able to financially support 45 members of staff to participate in the programme formally.

In years 1 and 2 of the programme, I could predict those wishing to participate and give a list of names. However, sitting here halfway through year 5, I genuinely cannot do that anymore. Our research programme is a dynamic and broad spectrum of interests and experiences that makes the outcomes all the richer. From those who have been with us 20 years, to those newly qualified and from those who may be managers and those that have a few hours teaching a week, this programme belongs to them all.

In 2022–2023, Allan Lasky, a Skills Improvement lecturer, conducted an action research project exploring the impact of food poverty on learner engagement. Year 1 of his work focused on the analysis of national data on food poverty, focus groups with learners and staff and visits to other FE institutions to explore the scale of the problem. At the end of year 1, Allan presented his work and a series of recommendations to relevant members of the senior leadership team in order to propose a series of evidence informed actions to start to address the issue. Allan is now running a college-based Cooking Club for learners that provides all learners that join with free ingredients to cater for four to five people and a recipe card. *It's not just about cheap food, it's about finding fresh, nutritious food and creating interesting recipes and meals within a budget. I'm really pleased with the uptake and feedback so far and would encourage more students to join us as the club is also helping to feed the families of students too, who may be struggling with the cost of living* (Lasky, 2023).

8.4 Methodology

The programme is designed to last the full academic year with each member of staff released from teaching for two hours a week. These are funded hours and dedicated space and time. These hours belong to the staff and they have agency over how and when to use them. The hours are not tracked, but clear expectations are set for the quality of the output by the end of the year.

Staff submit project proposals, and constructive feedback is provided by a panel who support the project development from the outset. Creativity is nurtured, and staff are able to take their project in the direction they feel is relevant to their practice; they are able to decide the focus, the methodology and the nature of the outcomes.

Through one-to-one support, the staff have ownership over how the project will evolve and adapt as new learning is acquired. This freedom of choice was essential so that staff felt motivated to explore areas of intrigue and not predetermined but leadership led agendas.

This programme is supported throughout the organisation from senior leadership team through to curriculum managers. All applications are submitted with line manager support, but the programme is designed to have a 'bottom up' and 'grassroots' approach so the staff have full ownership over the topic and direction of their work. This is an essential component of our ethos and one that our Senior Leadership team has fully embraced.

Commencing in the September, in addition to the two-hour release from teaching, the staff engage in a guest speaker and in-house workshop programme to develop the key research skills in line with the action research cycle. These sessions are always skills focused and have a level of differentiation to allow staff to select sessions based on the skills they are looking to develop.

All staff have access to as many one-to-one sessions as needed to develop their specific skill set throughout the year and to feedback on the progress of their thinking. A recent addition is the partnership between the practitioners and a member of the senior leadership team relevant to their area of exploration. This has allowed staff to be supported by a staff member who can share specialist knowledge and skills, establish networking opportunities and who can make decisions. Key to a genuine action research culture is meaningful change which is dependent on a leadership team willing to listen and learn from others and use that learning to inform strategic decision-making. Amplifying the staff voice through working relationships with those that hold strategic responsibility ensures that they feel valued, have organisational impact and their thinking is used to 'Feed the Tree' (Jones, 2020).

As the year progresses, the staff capture their work in a Google site dedicated to the action research pathway. Each staff has a website page which is an open forum where staff are encouraged to be creative in the presentation of their work through blogs, vlogs, photos, presentations, toolkits, learner and staff voice interview soundbites and formal writing. These pages fully belong to the staff and serve as a springboard for others keen to apply the research to their own area of teaching and learning practice.

The programme culminates in our annual Festival of Practice. With live music, catering and plant and book swaps, this has become a staple opportunity to celebrate a 'year of research' and more importantly the thinking of our staff. This large scale, two-day event is entirely focused on championing and sharing the work of all those on the programme. The festival sessions are workshop driven, and staff across the organisation can select sessions they would like to attend based on their own curiosity. The sessions are interactive and encourage those attending to consider how the ideas explored can be embedded into their own areas of practice. We encourage our researcher to share their work in one of two ways either as a product to handover to their peers or as a process 'focus group' to challenge their work and thinking to date. This gives the researchers the freedom to ensure that these workshops are useful to both themselves and their peers.

In 2022–2023, Alex Huggett, the Curriculum Head of Lifelong Learning, was inspired by the work of Rachel Arnold and her research work into 'Teach the Teacher'. Alex spent the year working with Rachel and implementing her findings into Alex's own day-to-day teaching and learning practice. Alex, who is an English teacher, found herself during the course of the academic year, being taught how to muck out stables with the equine learners, cooking with the caterers and wallpapering with construction. Alex shared her work at our 2023 Festival of Practice which led to six more lecturers taking on the 'Teach the Teacher' methodology in 2023–2024. The motivation and passion for this project resulted in the lecturers traveling to visit Rachel in Solihull College in December 2023 in order to network, witness the impact of the approach and learn how the work can be scaled up further.

> This has only made us keener to roll out this project at college – the potential to develop such vital relationships, build learner confidence and empower learners through this role reversal has extensive potential benefits in the skills classroom.
>
> (Huggett, 2024)

8.5 Findings and conclusions

We are now in year 5 of Culture of Curiosity, and year on year the programme is growing, becoming more embedded in our language and reaching more staff. However, we are still very much learning and always look at ways to improve its relevance to the staff, the institution and our wider college community.

So far, our findings have helped us to be sure that in order to establish a meaningful and sustainable action research culture needs to:

1 be built on genuine trust,
2 enhance the learning of both learners and staff,
3 encourage internal and external collaboration,
4 be inclusive and value the voice of all
5 be rooted in informed risk taking,
6 be driven by leadership support,
7 establish a language that challenges traditional negative assumptions on the nature of research and who can do it,
8 have space and time and to genuinely 'feed the tree' (Jones, 2020) rather than be rolled out quickly. It won't happen overnight,

9 champion the thinking of all staff and focused on the implementation of appropriate and relevant recommendations,
10 support practitioners to create robust and relevant impact measures to determine the success of the research and its potential to have wider college impact.

This list is not definitive. We still have so much to learn, and we have new areas we are 'curious' to explore. However, we are confident that these key findings give organisations that are keen to establish their own research cultures a place to start the journey rooted in tried and tested experience.

Due to the success of the Action Research Pathway and our acquired learning, we have now developed a much wider bespoke pathway approach to professional learning with the development of our 'Pathways of Curiosity' (see Figure 8.1). Continuing to be Springboarded from the reflective process

Figure 8.1 A Framework for Curiosity: The Journey of Coleg Sir Gar Coleg Ceredigion action researcher

of the self-evaluation and professional discussions, staff can opt to follow a much broader range of pathway themes for an academic year from EdTech, Industry Upskilling and Bilingualism through to Aspiring Leaders and Leadership Development.

In 2019 and 2022, we were proudly awarded the Princess Royal Training Award which was followed with a Cultural Pioneer Award in 2023 for our Culture of Curiosity. These awards are testament to our staff and our learners who are the reason that the programme has worked and continues to grow. Our recognition as Cultural Pioneers has brought us to a point of reflection on the programme to date and has given us the confidence to explore a new, more collaborative and ambitious version of this programme for September 2025.

8.6 Examples of culture in practice

8.6.1 *Cameras on/cameras off by Catherine Roberts*

March 2020 saw a monumental shift in how practitioners engage with the students. An exclusively online approach was a new, yet exciting prospect for practitioners. Initially, our college policy was that all students followed their normal face-to-face timetable but on our online platform. The policy outlined rules for engagement, which included staff and students having their cameras on in order to 'assess engagement'. The action research work of Catherine Roberts questioned how we measure engagement in online lessons and the effects of screen stress and anxiety on our students. The thought-provoking research concluded that 'physical' presence in online space was a simplistic way to measure engagement. Her conclusions outlined that engagement can be measured in several ways. A camera is not necessarily one of those ways, rather the use of real-time online tools such as the raise hand function, Google Chat, Jamboards and polls were a better indicator of student understanding and interaction in the session.

Catherine presented her research at our Festival of Practice. Staff received it positively and got them to question their own practice. Catherine also published her research in the national publication 'Intuition' (Roberts, 2021) which generated much questioning and discussion amongst the Twitter community.

The research of Catherine Roberts supported our college's change in policy surrounding online lessons. Students were encouraged to have their cameras on for an initial check-in, but during delivery, the students had autonomy to engage with their peers and lecturer in a way that they felt best suited. Whether that be through speech, emojis or chat functions within the session. Catherine's work encourages senior leaders, staff and students to rethink their approach to online lessons.

8.6.1.1 Project impact

This work fundamentally changed our college-wide perspective to how we wanted our learners to engage in the online space. This work was crucial in helping us to understand the dynamics of an online environment and ensure that we supported all learners to engage in a way that was comfortable for them and their individual needs. This work was our first article in the Intuition Publication for the Society for Education and Training on behalf of the Research College Group.

8.6.2 Online art exhibition by Karl Sedgwick

Curiosity is integral to art and design, and the pandemic highlighted this further. Exhibitions culminate in the ending of a degree or an art FE course. However, when the pandemic hit, the traditional physical exhibition wasn't possible.

The students were working to finish their projects whilst being locked down, so the only equipment that was available to them was that found in their local setting. Karl Sedgwick used his research project to explore and experiment with platforms and technology that would allow the learners to still share and celebrate their work on a large scale under these challenging conditions.

With the support of Karl's work, staff turned their minds to the virtual world; 3D scanning, photographing and video capturing art works to build an entire exhibition virtually, using 360 immersive spaces.

With the expertise of our staff to support this mammoth virtual exhibition, in 2020 nearly 40,000 visitors have seen the work, with nearly 20,000 visiting the 2021 exhibition.

Not only did this challenge traditional norms of what constitutes an exhibition, but pushed the boundaries of our staff through action research to support the development and the continued development of this extended platform. Following the pandemic, the future exhibitions will be both physical and digital, utilising the virtual skills developed. Using a 360 camera, the exhibition will be digitalised with 3D scanned objects for the extended community to see again.

8.6.2.1 Project impact

All learners could complete their year with a demonstration of the work that they had completed during lockdown. Even during the middle of a pandemic, the college and staff could celebrate and share the work on a much larger scale than in previous years. This was an incredibly ambitious project that fully met our objectives to empower staff, challenge the assumptions of what is and isn't possible and share their practice on a national platform.

References

Daniels, A. (2019) Application for princess royal training award. Unpublished: Coleg Sir Gar.

Huggett, A. (2024) Tutors visit Solihull for lessons delivered by students. Available at: https://www.colegsirgar.ac.uk/index.php/en/news/3809-tutors-visit-solihull-for-lessons-delivered-by-students [Accessed: 27 September 2024].

Jones, S. (2020) How to put teacher-led research at the heart of FE. *TES FE*, 26 April 2020. Available at: https://www.tes.com/magazine/archive/how-put-teacher-led-research-heart-fe [Accessed: 20 November 2023].

Lasky, A. (2023) Budget-friendly nutrition: college's culinary learning programme. Available at: https://www.colegsirgar.ac.uk/index.php/en/news/3858-budget-friendly-nutrition-college-s-culinary-learning-programme [Accessed: 27 September 2024].

Roberts, C. (2021) 'Facing the camera', *InTuition*, (46), pp. 37–39.

Chapter 9

The progress of research and scholarship in Scottish colleges
Charting some key developments

Patrick O'Donnell and Christine Calder

Despite claims of the increasing blurring of the boundaries between UK further education colleges (FECs) and universities (Feather, 2010, 2012; Medcalf, 2014; Orr, 2020; Scott, 2010), the positionality of research and scholarly activities can be held up as a well-established departure between the two sectors. While research and scholarship has always been a foremost feature of the core identity of the university, it has never been part of the core character, mindset and identity of FECs. And yet, in very recent years, we have witnessed a modest but nevertheless, steady interest in research and scholarly activities unfolding within Scottish colleges. This chapter explores this emerging research and scholarship dynamic within the Scottish further education (FE) setting.

9.1 Research question

The chapter seeks to reveal the sorts of dynamics that have created conditions for research and scholarly activities to emerge within the Scottish college sector and as such, it addresses the following broad question:

> *Why have research and scholarly activities become more visible within the Scottish FE context?*

To attend to the potential structural and cultural complexities, the main research question was further broken down into two sub-questions:

1. What traditional and cultural dynamics have influenced the research capacity building within Scotland's colleges?
2. What recent initiatives have emerged to open a space for research and scholarly activities to become more discernible within Scotland's colleges?

9.2 Positionality

At a time when Scottish colleges are suffering from financial instability, this research provided an opportune moment to pause and consider why we are at such an interesting time for research in colleges. It truly feels like it is a movement that is gaining traction, and we are genuinely interested to consider why research in FE has evolved and is currently evolving in the manner that it is.

Our positionality is key here, and we recognise that we resonate, in part, to Bourke's (2014) work when he suggests that positionality is a space where 'objectivism and subjectivism meet'. Considering such sentiments, we both strive to be as objectively curious as possible when undertaking this project, happily challenging each other's biases, while respectfully acknowledging our own particular biographical backgrounds. We share many interests, but above all we both are actively involved in research in the college sector and therefore, starting this project from a position where we have a vested interest to reveal new trends in FE such as the emergence of research, an activity that sits outside the traditional work of FECs.

Patrick works for a Scottish college that has for the last three decades been a major academic partner of what can be described as a geographically dispersed dual sector (FE/HE) institution: the university of the Highlands and Islands (an institution that will be unpacked in more details later). For Patrick, the topic of research culture and research capacity building within university and FECs is no stranger, and he has published on the evolution of research within education and has embraced the role of research coordinator for a number of years within his own institution. As such, he has an intimate understanding of sorts of challenges and rewards associated with building research capacity in a dual sector FE/HE institution.

Christine works in a large Scottish college with a remit that covers teacher training as well as professional learning, and she is a passionate advocate for research in, on and for the college sector. To this end, she regularly collaborates with colleagues across Scotland and the four nations to encourage the growth of research in FE. Action research and participatory action research are particular areas of interest for Christine as she believes both offer an opportunity to focus on critical praxis for individuals, groups or institutions. With action research findings having the potential to be usable to many, she firmly believes that there is significant potential for increasingly using action research in the college sector as a mechanism to aid positive change.

Our hope is that the following text not only charts and documents a moment in time but also, and crucially, offers the possibility for readers to envisage what research expansion in Scottish colleges might mean for the sector and beyond.

9.3 Fostering research and scholarship within the FE sector: mapping structural and cultural barriers

Discussions surrounding the widespread scarcity of research and scholarly activities within FECs can be traced back three decades. Rowley (1996, p. 75) considered the tension between research activities and teaching in FE, observing that heavy teaching commitments meant that teaching staff had little time to conduct meaningful research and scholarship. Elliott (1996) claimed that the collective world of FE does not have a research culture and, with the exception of a limited number of self-motivated and dedicated individuals, is not engaged in research of an exploratory nature. Elliott (1996, p. 107) also makes clear that the core delivery activities and associated management practices embedded within the FE sector frustrated the nurturing of research within the FE college:

> [...] the current priorities and operational pressures of FE, especially those arising from managerialist agendas, may be seen as a highly effective ideological device for neutralising the development of a research culture.

In a follow-up article entitled 'Why Research is Still Invisible in Further Education', Solvason and Elliott (2013) reveal that the 'ideological devices' for preventing the development of research and scholarly activities have not diminished over time. They observe 'a college culture that is antithetic to thoughtful reflection and research'. Similarly, Young (2002) examined those teaching HE in FE and argued how the idea of academic prowess and scholarship are not particularly valued by college management. According to Young (2002), this was manifested by a career promotional structure that placed skills in human resource management and budget management well above the sorts of academic and scholarly abilities (skills sets) that underpin research activities. Others such as Feather's (2010, 2012) study on academic identity amongst lecturers delivering HE in FECs reveals that 'teaching', 'scholarship' and 'research' are the 'holy trinity' underpinning academics' identity within universities. Making the comparison between FECs and universities, Feather (2010, 2013) observed that college lecturers traditionally have heavy teaching commitments and a wide portfolio of taught subjects. Consequently, they have limited opportunity to both conduct research and scholarship that fosters deeper critical insights into their subject area(s) and are also unlikely to find the time outside a busy teaching timetable to cultivate research collaborations with colleagues from other colleges or university academic staff.

Within the Scottish FE sector context, the lack of a research profile and culture has long been recognised. During a 2007 conference on Scottish FE, the potential benefits of introducing research and scholarship activities within Scottish FECs were discussed. The then Depute Chief Executive of the Scottish Further Education Unit, John McCann (2007) rejected what he termed tokenism in respect of research activities and called for a well-coordinated and holistic approach to developing research activities within the Scottish FEC sector: 'all parties need to work together – it is not about "researchers" and "non-researchers" – research needs to become part of the educational landscape rather than being regarded as something that is nice to have as an additional extra'.

The cultural and structural dynamics that impede research activities within Scottish colleges were also teased out in the conference by the keynote speaker Professor David James (2007):

> If a research culture is to be established in Scotland's colleges, then it is important to acknowledge that there are difficulties. The subject level, physical and psychological 'silos' need to be broken down. Further, the promotion of research requires leadership that has vision and future planning, and management (how to get there) instead of managerialism. Managerialism is premised on the idea that the manager already has all the answers.

Not only did James' (2007) keynote speech helpfully introduce us to the sorts of *physical and psychological 'silos'* to overcome, but he also makes us contemplate the fundamental question: *Why should the FE sector be encouraged to conduct research?* Attending to this question, perhaps the most compelling arguments relate to the FE sector's positionality and expanding remit. The FE college's most striking feature is its diversity, reach and the distinctive contribution it makes to the local economies and to advancing social inclusion imperatives. Moreover, over the last two decades, the FE landscape has been fast-evolving, subject to a flood of new policy reforms seeking to expand the sector's role and mission. Consequently, it is fair to say the FE landscape has evolved to become a rich field for exploration, and those working within the sector are ideally placed to explore their working environment and the impact of FE education reform.

But of course, Scottish colleges like the rest of the UK FE have long operated with a performativity script and education policy imperatives that conflict with the concept of FE-based research activities. The monitoring, regulating and judgment process linked to the enactment of educational reform objectives have been described by Ball (2003, 2013) as the encroaching discourse of performativity. The discourse of performativity is said to mark out and stress key institutional aims and policy imperatives. Critically, performativity discourse influences how individuals and groups are inscribed in and respond to the officially sanctioned policy reform imperatives. In this sense, educational policy and performance indicators can be perceived as an 'enactment script', assigning particular roles and identities for educational sectors. The FE performativity discourse, so our argument follows, offers a helpful lens to understand why research and scholarship has not found a firm foothold in FECs. Under the FE performativity scripts, teaching delivery is the core activity and as such, there is a natural scepticism towards anything that is perceived to be detached from the established working parameters and prescribed core activities. Accordingly, under our FE performativity, college lecturers are firmly identified as teachers, facilitators of learning and interpreters/translators/decoders of existing knowledge/understandings, and the concept of lecturers conducting research would be perceived as unwarranted distraction from the traditional teaching role.

9.4 Existing context: pushing against the grain of tradition – recent initiatives that foster research and scholarly activities within Scottish FE colleges

As touched upon earlier, research and scholarship that has been long held up has one of the quintessential differences between universities and FECs. However, in recent times within the Scottish context, this long-held position underscoring the distinction between universities and colleges has been somewhat unsettled by two separate initiatives pursuing the mutual goal to foster a research culture within Scottish FECs:

1 The establishment of Scottish Dual HE and FE University – University of the Highlands and Islands (UHI)
2 The expansion to the remit (to include research) of a government body specifically set up to support Scottish FE colleges – referred to as College Development Network (CDN)

9.5 University of the Highlands and Islands

In August 2011, the University of the Highlands and Islands (UHI) celebrated the accolade of university title, becoming Scotland's newest university. Modelled on a federal, collegiate university based on a number of existing and geographically dispersed FE colleges and research institutions, the UHI has clearly abandoned the more conventional model of a single campus university in a single location. Although the UHI achieved university status in 2011, its existence as an HE institution can be traced back to 2001, and at the time of writing, the Scottish FE sector comprises 24 colleges, seven of which are part of the UHI partnership. The UHI FE colleges are commonly known as Academic Partners (APs) and deliver a wide range of HE.

From the outset, the desire to foster a research culture became an overarching theme within the UHIs Strategic Planning Framework documents and the ensuing years (starting from early 2000 to onwards) ushered in a number of policies and initiatives specifically geared towards the building research capacity within the partnership. By way of example, UHI Executive Office (EO) requested that all UHI partners to draw up their own research strategies, setting up research committees to encourage, co-ordinate and support research and scholarly activities that both align broadly with the aims of the UHI EO Research Strategy and also reflect their own individual institutional strengths, opportunities and interests. The UHI has also a research office which provides support and advice to all the partner institutions.

Encouraged by the new emphasis placed on research by the UHI Executive, a number of the FE colleges (APs) established their own research units and centres employing full-time researchers to kick-start a research profile within their institutions. Many of these colleges-based researchers also teach at postgraduate master's and PhD level (within their research subject area), and thus, they are seen as part of the college teaching community as well as an active researcher. The UHI EO also introduced a number of important initiatives to build research capacity throughout the partnership. These included the provision of financial support and guidance for existing and newly created research projects and institutions, the introduction of a sabbatical scheme for all UHI staff wishing to pursue scholarship and research. Moreover, the UHI created a Learning and Teaching Academy (LTA) that administers a range of funding streams and support to help staff develop their professional practice and engage in research. These funding streams include scholarship fund (for individuals and teams to undertake research), research conference fund (supports staff attending research conferences) and staff development fund for research training. Significantly, the UHI LTA provides an important focal point and physical space for staff to come together and network and collaborate on research and professional development.

Over the years, the UHI EO strategic planning imperatives for research capacity building have steadily diffused outwards introducing a particular university performativity discourse and script that supports, values and encourages research within the partner colleges.

The current UHI strategy stresses the importance of research through several aims and goals including:

Creating a vibrant research environment which builds on our collective strengths, supports innovation and creates opportunities for interdisciplinary activity.
Developing an institutional culture in which academic staff actively engage in research and scholarship that enhances curriculum quality and student experience.

A salient point to make here is that the policies and initiatives designed to encourage and expand research activities within the UHI partnership – seen as echoing the university performativity script for research capacity building – have been highly instrumental in mobilising and focusing partner colleges to appreciate that research(ers) and scholarly activities should be fully embedded. To be clear, such research capacity building interventions have not shifted the emphasis away from teaching, rather they have pushed research and scholarly activities to become enshrined in the partner colleges strategic planning documents, creating the necessary conditions whereby research activities would no longer be a matter of individual pursuit but rather be part of the collective interest to the wider UHI organisation.

9.6 College Development Network

Scotland has a number of government-funded bodies that have a remit to support colleges, and these include the CDN, a training and development body, primarily funded by the Scottish Funding Council. The very recent launch of the CDN Research and Enhancement Centre (2020) can be seen as an important flagship initiative aiming to encourage and support research and scholarship within the Scottish college sector. CDN's Research and Enhancement Centre has become the base for what it terms associate researchers from FECs and beyond. These associate researchers, who are college and university researchers, have the opportunity to network together, develop and share their research interests; thus, they are important actors in fostering research activities within the FECs. The Research and Enhancement Centre has also introduced initiatives such as The Step Forward Researcher Development Programme which delivers a series of workshops and researcher meet-ups which are led by members of the Research Enhancement Centre, their associates and occasional guests. These sessions are specifically aimed to support college staff (open to both teaching and support staff) to develop the skills required to undertake research projects that will enhance their own practice and improve outcomes for their college and its learners. The Research and Enhancement Centre also commissions research projects, within their pool of associate researchers, which in turn supports FE-based researchers to continue to hone, refresh or develop their own research skills. It is difficult to oversell the progressive character of the CDN Research and Enhancement Centre and the major impact it has on encouraging and supporting research with the Scottish colleges. Indeed, the CDNs efforts here are instrumental in making research part of the role and identity of an FE college. A clear indicator of its aspiration to have a wide-ranging impact can be seen in its very recent launching of a research journal for Scottish FE colleges. The peer-reviewed journal, referred to as *College Action Inquiry Research Network (CAIRN)*, provides a valuable forum to disseminate innovation, knowledge and critical insights through a variety of scholarly submissions by those within or working with the Scottish FE sector. It's also important to point out that the recent flood of educational policy for Scottish tertiary education has been accompanied by the appeal for evidence-based research to inform and legitimise policy direction, and against this setting, CAIRN is a timely enterprise, particularly, if it disseminates scholarly articles that provide new insights on FE operation and impact. Although the work of CDN's Research Enhancement Centre is still in its infancy, the production of published college-based literature has unlimited potential. It offers the opportunity to provide clear evidence around the breadth and depth of work of Scottish Colleges which is currently out of scope of policy makers and influencers, whilst also aiding colleges to keep progressing away from performativity and towards an education system that operates with true social justice values at its core, for all.

9.7 Methodology

The contents of this chapter were derived from a desk-based approach, where we reviewed some of the papers available, primarily via the internet and available in peer-reviewed research journals. This is a form of empirical research, where you gather your own data, but the data gathered for this project utilises secondary data that has already been written and published. Researching in this manner has many positives such as being low cost and low risk, and it allows the researchers to bring together information/themes/data identified from a diverse array of studies into one paper. What was apparent however was the scarcity of published literature available based on research in Scottish colleges.

9.8 Findings

In Scotland, we have seen a modest but steady shift in attitudes towards embedding research and scholarly activities within FECs. The UHI has been highly instrumental here in creating conditions where its APs are discursively engaging with what can be seen as research-orientated performativity script; one that is geared towards building research capacity. Within the UHI APs, the concept of staff securing remitted time from teaching duties to conduct (and publish research) is not seen as an unconventional activity but part of an overarching concerted effort to build research capacity.

The setting up of CDN's Research and Enhancement Centre (2020) is highly noteworthy as it heralds a palpable recognition from officialdom that the Scottish FE sector should have an opportunity to engage in research and build a research profile through networking with each other. Thus, while we recognise that teaching has long been the core dominant activity in Scottish FE, firmly utilised to define, justify and celebrate the FE sectors wider social and economic contribution, the new drive by CDN's Research and Enhancement Centre to cultivate research and scholarship activities with Scottish colleges holds the very real promise of opening a space for colleges to add and celebrate research activities to their core activities and mission.

9.9 Conclusion

Under FE's performativity script, college lecturers are firmly identified as teachers, facilitators of learning and interpreters/translators of existing knowledge and understanding. Indeed, by virtue of adhering to their own FE performativity scripts (set by policy makers), FECs will not have the incentives to be concerned with research and associated scholarly activities.

But if we return to the main research question, why have research and scholarly activities become more visible in the college sector? We posit research has become more visible because of undertakings from institutions such as the UHI and CDN as well as innovative FE-based thinkers, leaders and of course FE-based researchers, who have the vision and drive to push beyond the boundaries of FE's traditional performativity script.

We now invite you, the reader, to reflect on what the future could hold if these modest origins of research and scholarly activities in colleges were to gain more traction and more visibility. It would be valuable to consider here what the effect might be for students, staff, and colleges and what this might mean for broader society.

References

Ball, S. (2013) *The education debate.* 2nd edn. Bristol: Policy Press.

Ball, S. J. (2003) 'The teacher's soul and the terrors of performativity', *Journal of Education Policy*, 8(2), p. 215228.

Bourke, B. (2014) 'Positionality: reflecting on the research process', *The Qualitative Report*, 19(33), pp. 1–9.

Elliott, G. (1996) 'Why is research invisible in further education?', *British Educational Research Journal*, 22(1), pp. 101–111.

Feather, D. (2010) 'A whisper of academic identity: an HE in FE perspective', *Research in Post-Compulsory Education*, 15(2), pp. 189–204. doi: 10.1080/13596741003790740.

Feather, D. (2012) 'Do lecturers delivering higher education in further education desire to conduct research?', *Research in Post-Compulsory Education*, 17(3), pp. 335–347.

James, D. (2007) 'Research in FE: a distraction from core business or a royal road to Improvement? Why research matters', Research Conference, SFEU, Argyll Court, Stirling, 9th May.

McCann, J. (2007) 'Enhancing Quality Through Research', paper presented at Research Conference, SFEU, Argyll Court, Stirling, 9th May.

Medcalf, R. (2014) 'Research and scholarship in a 'HE in FE' environment', *Journal of Hospitality, Leisure, Sport & Tourism Education*, 15, pp.11–19. doi: https://doi.org/10.1016/j.jhlste.2014.03.001.

Orr, K. (2020) 'A future for the further education sector in England', *Journal of Education and Work*, 33(7–8), pp. 507–514. doi: 10.1080/13639080.2020.1852507.

Rowley, J. (1996) 'Making the tension between research and teaching creative in business and management: a pilot study', *Journal of Further and Higher Education*, 20(1), pp. 74–92.

Scott, G. (2010) 'Delivering higher education within further education in England: issues, tensions and opportunities', *Management in Education*, 24(3), pp. 98–101. http://dx.doi.org/10.1177/0892020608090409

Solvason, C. and Elliott, G. (2013) 'Why is research still invisible in further education', *Journal of Learning Development in Higher Education*, (6). doi: 10.47408/jldhe.v0i6.206.

Young, P. (2002) 'Scholarship is the word that dare not speak its name: lecturers' experiences of teaching on a higher education programme in a further education college', *Journal of Further and Higher Education*, 26(3), pp. 273–286.

Chapter 10

The power of community

Developing intergenerational learning spaces

Fey Cole

My vocational area is Early Years. Working with young children, one develops an awareness of the vital connection between research and learning. Consider the child engaging in exploratory play, making sense of the way the season has changed: the leaves from green to red; the snail leaving evidence of his journey with a shiny trail; the puddle reaching close to the top of the wellington boot. As we transition through educational systems, we can find ourselves forgetting the importance of curiosity for developing our minds and knowledge acquisition. My research has led me to explore the significance of exploring our curiosities in the Further Education (FE) environment.

My name is Fey Cole, and I currently work as a Curriculum Manager in a Further and Higher Education college in Northern Ireland in the Department of Health, Life, and Personal Sciences. After working in the Early Years sector, I moved to a lecturing position in 2011, finding a role that stimulated my own curiosity and brought me much joy as I worked alongside employers to bring out the best from students entering a sector that means a great deal to me. Now in a leadership position, I view it as a duty to role model the expectations I ask of others. This includes being committed to life-long learning and being actively involved in research projects that enhance the provision we offer and the learning experiences for students.

10.1 Research questions

The research undertaken adopted a multifaceted approach as it progressed. It began with me undertaking an action research project on how students having ownership of their learning journey impacted their well-being and educational outcomes. A series of questionnaires were completed by students to evaluate the correlation between students' engagement and emotive responses towards activities, with their responses to learning tasks and summative educational outcomes. It then progressed to my own academic research for my master's dissertation, analysing how project-based learning can enhance the vocational classroom.

Both the action and dissertation research was undertaken in a large-scale project-based learning (PBL) activity that ran through the length of the academic year. Students on their second year of their course led an 'intergenerational cafe' to complete elements of different units they were studying, and the sessions were designed to develop students' skills and evaluate the learning taking place by children attending (a key component of their Early Years qualification). This allowed for me to review their evidence of learning with previous students and with this cohort's year one work to evaluate how the approach had influenced their final portfolio submissions.

The University and College Union's (UCU) report 'Transformative Teaching and Learning in Further Education' (Duckworth and Smith, 2019) highlights the benefits of educators in FE engaging with research and discusses how the correlation of values between an educator and the values of their research provides conditions to nurture hope and work towards social justice, an important part of the identity of the research I was undertaking. The intergenerational project was one where students connected with the wider community and adopt a social action approach. Students observing the educator as a learner created an environment where we worked together and felt confident in sharing our reflections as we progressed. This was beneficial for my research as supported me to gain insightful reflections from students as to how the different components of the intergenerational PBL activities were impacting their learning experience (Cole, 2022). Throughout the project, I focused on the impact student autonomy had on outcomes as they designed, implemented, and evaluated the intergenerational café, in line with their own learning outcomes for their qualification.

10.2 Positionality

My action research influenced how integrated values were as the projects developed. The values of play, community, and kindness underpin my own teaching practice and shape the way in which I develop projects and interact with others. Feeling a sense of belonging influences how secure we feel to be ourselves, and my hope was to be able to capture how vital knowing who we are and feeling secure supports us in becoming life-long learners. Recognising the importance of creating a democratic, thoughtful, and sustainable learning environment, it was important to embed the UN Sustainable Goal of Global Citizen. The 'Transforming Our World: The 2030 Agenda for Sustainable Development' (United Nations, 2015) largely shaped the positionality of the research, with consideration as to how the educational experience fed into the values of being a global citizen.

When wanting to develop pedagogical approaches where students influence the way that learning experiences are designed, we need to look critically at how we ensure the learning space is one that reflects them and actively listens to what they have to say. Analysing these values placed me on a path

Intergenerational Learning Spaces 113

to connect my values with the research I was undertaking. These values and this approach became even more embedded when working with the extended community through intergenerational projects; we needed to establish what were our common values and how they should shape the experience.

Northern Ireland has become a much more diverse country than it was one decade ago. When bringing people together for the project, it was vital to be aware that there came many different experiences and links to a history that is unique compared to other parts of the United Kingdom. We know how negatively impacting The Troubles still are on generations who have been raised following the Good Friday Agreement, and the recent report 'It didn't end in 1998' (McAlister et al., 2021) outlines that we should recognise the impact of the transgenerational legacy of the years of violence and develop safe spaces within educational systems, alongside being aware of our own bias when discussing this area of history. The report recommends a two-generation approach to learning about the conflict. Our focus was not primarily on this area but with generations together, and with us reviewing our collective future as a community, it was important to recognise and know how to respond to these types of discussions.

Something that shaped my own approach was listening to older people share their stories of the influence of the FE college in shaping their experiences growing up. Where schools and community organisations were segregated throughout The Troubles in Northern Ireland, the 'Tech' was somewhere that was open to everyone and brought people with different religions together for the first time. With the value of integrity, I see it as FE's duty to continue to be proactive in responding to the needs of every student and to create a space that is welcoming for all, with the opportunity to discuss differences in a safe and caring environment. To thrive, we need to feel the security of belonging.

10.3 Using knowledge

Finding existing research proved more problematic, as there was limited literature on intergenerational learning within the FE environment. As a result, I began to build on my research as part of writing two books on these areas of learning. Throughout my research on project-based learning (Cole, 2024), I found that this is often an approach adopted in more affluent school systems, with students from working class areas still working with systems that have not shifted much since the school system was first introduced. There seems to be a reluctance for individuals to be able to *move lanes* rather than conforming to the path laid out before them. This was one reason why I wanted to show how it works in a vocational college, with a diverse representation of students.

For our intergenerational sessions, we did not want to add to student's workload but ensure that PBL was adopted as a pedagogical approach as part of the course design. There was limited research on this approach, but intergenerational learning has become more recognised over recent years, and I was able to evaluate research from across the globe which has used this method effectively, mainly undertaken in Asia and America (Duke et al., 2021). Aware that intergenerational spaces have been identified by the UK Government to implement further in the coming years (House of Lords Library, 2019). It was an important area of focus to ensure it is embedded effectively and purposefully in the future.

10.4 Methodology

The research participants initially were students working towards a level three vocational diploma in Early Years, as well as Foundation Degree students studying Health and Social Care. There were a lot of ethical considerations to consider in the studies as consent and understanding of the project were very important, and I had to ensure that this was explained and disseminated age appropriately, limiting crossovers of information. While it would have been useful to video record parts of the project, this was limited to prevent its impact on the interactions between generations, and interviews and feedback were the main way of collecting data. Focus groups with the 16- to 19-year-olds were hosted to delve deeper into the experiences, alongside evaluations of tasks that they participated in to review how the sessions had impacted their coursework approach.

I was aware that the research was an emergent and responsive project and the shared process of reflection was an important feature at each stage. A participatory approach meant our action research was co-produced between educators and students to break down the power dynamics that can be felt within the more traditional classroom and ensure it empowered both parties to take ownership and feel confident to truly reflect on their experiences and effectively evaluate the findings so that these could inform our practice for moving forward. Regular questionnaires that focused on well-being supported us in our studies to analyse how we responded emotionally to different learning environments and strategies. Similar questionnaires were used in our more typical lessons, as well as in spaces where the new pedagogical approaches had been implemented.

The methods continued to be developed, with more detailed analysis of grade trends prior and during the projects. Written or audio/video reflective journals, from lecturers and students, were reviewed and informed our understanding of how the intergenerational space was influencing how we approached our learning and teaching experience. The strong partnerships with all stakeholders supported us in evaluating how students interacted with learning opportunities and extended knowledge acquisition. McClintock et al. (2014) suggest that individuals need to vocalise their thoughts to another person to gain a more in-depth personal reflection, which in turn leads to improvements in comprehension. Within the intergenerational sessions, storytelling and dialogue were a strong part of the sessions, and this style of research methodology provided capacity to map emotions and comprehension in the storytelling environment.

10.5 Findings

During the studies, it was evident that the experience was having a much larger impact on the positive mental health and self-confidence of students than I had expected. In pre-experience surveys, 35% of students rated their emotional response at the end of a lesson as being 'good' or 'very good'. In week 12, the percentage of students feeling 'good' or 'very good' raised to 68%, and in week 16 it progressed to 78%. This could be down to their development as they grew more confident in the classroom, but the same survey was undertaken in classes they completed in more traditional lectures, and we did not see a lift than more than 62% in responses. By tracking emotional responses to the learning environment, we observed a vast shift in the mindset of students engaged with the projects, and in interview and reflection sessions, students frequently engaged in dialogue independently on how the time spent in an intergenerational environment left them feeling happier and more appreciative of the purpose of what they were doing. During these interviews, 86% of students discussed a greater appreciation of learning and 92% felt more connected to their community. This brought higher learner experience satisfaction. It was evident that the intergenerational space was increasing students' sense of belonging and connecting them with the wider community.

The intergenerational project was initially implemented for a year and is now an integral part of our curriculum delivery. Intergenerational, project-based learning activities are written into the curriculums' scheme of work, with students using the intergenerational approach. Working closely with employers, we evaluated how the skills being used in the project-based learning classes enhanced the employability skills for moving into the workforce and they supported me to design the schemes of work and lesson plans for the project to ensure that key skills were incorporated that students would require for future employment. In questionnaires completed by employers, 58% reported that they had seen students' leadership skills develop and 62% had found that students communication skills had developed. Four employers had implemented their own intergenerational projects, with students integral to their implementation in the workplace. The projects reflected 21st century skills and adopted sustainable methods wherever possible, to enhance students' awareness of moving into a future workforce where a green economy is a key area of focus. Within final project portfolio submissions, 70% of students showed enhanced critical thinking skills and there was an 85% increase in collaboration. Student pre- and post-surveys identified that their awareness of green economy concepts had risen by 35%.

One of the reflective methods we incorporated was that of Kline's (2009) *Thinking Rounds*, and this method is now being used frequently within our classrooms following the research. Adopting this method for reflection was integral to qualitative research and ensured everyone's voice was heard. Actively working on our listening skills and ensuring that we all had the opportunity to reflect not only develops higher order thinking but also supports an environment where open and honest reflections are appreciated and celebrated by peers. Listening is one of the most powerful tools for creating safe learning spaces. If we can facilitate lessons where students recognise that the collective voice is the most powerful, we are developing the leaders we need for the future.

10.6 Findings throughout the two projects

There was a lot of interest in what we were doing, and we began hosting research events to promote a collaborative approach to researching and promoting the benefits of learning together, across areas and levels. Students and educators were working together, gaining a deeper sense of what we can learn from each other when researching side-by-side. As an educator, I pose the question to you, the reader, how often do you undertake the same activities as the students you work with? It brings valuable insight when we do this and commits us to being life-long learners ourselves, as we understand each component of the process and can appreciate how our emotions respond to the challenge of different activities. This was an important learning point for us from the research and we found that when students observed this role-modelling, they were much more forthcoming with their ideas for mapping the learning journey and speaking up when they had difficulties. Although this was not a focus of the studies, it was an unintended consequence that proved beneficial.

10.7 Conclusion

Action research is an evolving and beautiful journey to go on as a student and staff team. It connects us with our natural curiosity and develops and/or rekindles a love of learning. FE is the key space that connects learning with the economy, with multi-faceted pathways for students to progress onto their chosen profession. It is also a teaching environment where we roll up our sleeves and embrace 'messy' learning, which allows exploration and celebrates innovation. Our role as educators to serve and enhance our communities is a privileged position, and through action and professional research, we not only are able to raise the profile of the sector but we are also able to evidence how the innovative techniques in the classroom develop the skills of our future workforce and community.

Our research provided us with the evidence to look through a critical lens and take the opportunity to re-design lessons and ensure our curriculum schemes of work met with the current needs of both the sector and students, where both the individual and collective were at the heart of our delivery. My studies also led to me learning from educators across the globe and widened my perspectives. We need to look outwards if we want to remain innovative and be responsive to both local and global trends.

The pedagogical shift made learning more connected and purposeful through the incorporation of regular reflective sessions. Although mental health strategies were not formally integrated into lessons, it came naturally through the intergenerational space, and this gained positive results. Students excelled in their tasks, having greater autonomy regarding what happened over the course of the academic year. Sharing this journey will be useful for other educators and researchers, as it will identify how a creative approach to delivery can remove a power imbalance between the teacher and students, whilst also improving outcomes.

FE provision is in a prime position to connect students with the wider community, explore the correlation between academia and emotions, and embrace social action projects. In summary, I leave, you reader, with a question: do you truly know the individuals beside you in the classroom? Do you laugh, play, explore, and love what you do as a team? Maybe this is your opportunity to explore this further through the medium of active and responsive research, which is led by the collective curiosities.

References

Cole, F. (2022) *Intergenerational learning in schools and settings: an Educator's guide.* Oxen, England: Routledge Publication.

Cole, F. (2024) *An educator's guide to project-based learning: turning theory into practice.* Oxen, England: Routledge.

Duckworth, V. and Smith, R. (2019) *Transforming lives. Further education: finding hope.* London: UCU.

Duke, N.K., Halvorsen, A.-L., Strachan, S.L., Kim, J. and Konstantopoulos, S. (2021) 'Putting PBL to the test: the impact of project-based learning on second Graders' social studies and literacy learning and motivation in low-SES school settings', *American Educational Research Journal*, 58(1), pp. 160–200.

House of Lords Library. (2019) Tackling intergenerational unfairness [Online]. Available at: https://publications.parliament.uk/pa/ld201719/ldselect/ldintfair/329/329.pdf [Accessed: 29 September 2024].

Kline, N. (2009) *More time to think.* Pool-in-Wharfedale: Fisher King Pub.

McAlister, S., Corr, M. L., Dwyer, C. and Drummond, O. (2021) 'It didn't end in 1998': examining the impacts of conflict legacy across generations [Online]. Queen's University Belfast. Available at: https://www.qub.ac.uk/research-centres/CentreforChildrensRights/CCRFilestore/Filetoupload,1224477,en.pdf [Accessed: 29 September 2024].

McClintock, B., Pesco, D. and Martin-Chang, S. (2014) 'Thinking aloud: effects on text comprehension by children with specific language impairment and their peers', *International Journal of Language and Communication Disorders*, 49(6), pp. 637–648. http://onlinelibrary.wiley.com.libezproxy.open.ac.uk/doi/10.1111/1460-6984.12081/abstract

United Nations. (2015). Transforming our world: the 2030 agenda for sustainable development. https://documents.un.org/doc/undoc/gen/n15/291/89/pdf/n1529189.pdf [Accessed: 21 October 2015].

Chapter 11

Developing the capacity for, and use of, practitioner research

The Research College Group

Samantha Jones

11.1 Introduction: what is the Research College Group and how did it come about?

The Research College Group (RCG) was founded in 2020 and is an organisation which brings together organisations from across the post-16 sector to improve the visibility and use of practitioner research. The mission of the group is to inform and develop practice across all aspects of the operations of post-16 organisations, based primarily upon research from *within* the post-16 education and training sector. The group aims to develop the expertise, capacity, quality, and publication of research across the group of member organisations, and to collaborate on research and the delivery of projects, including those funded by third parties.

By 2024, the aim of the RCG was to have become recognised as a body whose sector-leading thinking shaped and developed research practice. It aimed to work for and with existing bodies, but under terms of parity, and sought to develop the profile and capacity of the post-16 education and training sector. In the longer term, the RCG intended to sustain itself financially through the funding generated by its research work. (Source: Research College Group – Founder Member Organisation Commitments.)

This chapter explores one of the externally funded projects undertaken by the RCG to bring to light how the principles and practices sought to achieve the mission and aims described above.

11.2 Research questions

The aim of the work was to identify good examples of English GCSE resit practice from within the sector. The research was undertaken to inform a suite of Continuous Professional Development (CPD) sessions for a third party working for the Department for Education (DfE). Methodologically, the decision was taken to include practitioner research, practice and theorisation as much as possible, both in the review of the literature and in the data collected on the teaching practices of participants. The intention of this approach was both to value practitioner knowledge in the development of sector practice and showcase new methodologies for the use of practitioner research. The reasoning of this approach was to place the Further Education (FE) teachers as the owners of their own knowledge. This perspective draws on Hordern's (2021, pp. 1458–1459) argument that 'it is not possible to make appropriate judgements about the practice without becoming a practitioner oneself. It is only if the researcher is committed to the practice, and identifies as a practitioner, that research can be fully attuned to the needs of the practice' and the argument of Chen et al. (2025) 'that practitioner-researchers not only have the capacity to produce high-quality research, but also may, at times, be the best researchers due to their experience of practice and their understanding of key issues in the field'.

11.3 Positionality

The section above sets out how we valued the knowledge and practice within the FE sector and how our position was as a largely independent body sitting outside the ownership of any one college, sixth form or adult education provider. Arguably, our values and our position were influenced by our community. As a group of individuals who both taught and researched in FE, we wanted to approach the research in a way that gave the status and recognition that is it argued that is lacking to the practitioner researchers from the sector (Chen et al., 2025). We also sought to develop the utility of the work to make it 'useful' (Lloyd and Jones, 2018) thereby giving a voice to the sector practitioners within the work developing of the sector. To do this, the practitioner work was *used in parity* with work that originated from other sectors, after all if the sector practitioners are the group who attend to the needs of a practice, in this case teaching GCSE re-sits in post-16 organisations, it seems logical that they have a voice in the development of the professional development that will go on to shape future practice. As we will see, this necessitated the continued development of methodologies and arguments to included FE teachers and researchers in shaping the practice within the sector.

11.4 Using knowledge

The chapter has already positioned the object under investigation, the research on practice by the practitioner, as lacking status but having the potential to give insight that is not able to be found elsewhere. This position is supported by Martell et al. (2021) who state that the voice of the practitioner is missing from the academic literature, which in turn impoverishes the knowledge of teaching within the sector.

The FE sector is generally considered to work within managerial constraints which results in those practitioner researchers working in the sector facing significant barriers such as funding, time, workload, access to journals, and access to conferences (Chen et al., 2025; Elliott, 1996). The lack of a research culture across the sector results in few organisations creating posts that allow practitioners to research as part of their role, which in turn compounds a lack of an understanding and value for the links between research and practice (Chen et al., 2025; Elliott, 1996; Richards, Lloyd and Donovan, 2023).

When disseminating work in the sector, language can be an issue. This is not to say that leaders and workers in the sector are not capable of reading complex language; it is more a reflection of the diversity of the sector. Each subject has its own accompanying language or voice (Bernstein, 2000) and not being familiar with the language or what can be legitimately communicated by a voice can 'lock people out' of a discussion. Atkins and Tummons (2017) argue that Teacher Education is a contentious site as it does not always give access to underpinning theory, and I would argue that reading this theory gives access to this language and voice of educational theory, allowing the sector's teachers to access wider thoughts and debates in the educational space, ignoring it limits what can be accessed and known. Therefore, if some, but not all staff, have access to a language or voice, there is an argument to be presented that there is a need to find ways of expressing these ideas in a way that is legitimate within the present norms of the sector.

Existing publications, in formal spaces such as this, evidence a rich seam of work that explores practitioner research written by those who support, teach, and facilitate the work (see Appleby and Hillier, 2012; Gregson, 2020; McNiff, Lomax and Whitehead, 2003). However, this work focuses on the use of the research work by the individual researchers, or discusses in theory how the work could be useful in other spaces, but does not explain how this could look in reality. The work of the RCG aims to address this gap.

11.5 The existing context

Sections 11.2 and 11.3 have already laid out some of the issues faced practically and theoretically in terms of the positionality of FE sector workers' ownership of, and access to, knowledge.

The existing market for CPD in this space is predominately run by third parties, and some of whom focus on knowledge from and of the FE sector and some whom to do not. Some trainers have never worked in the sector or may not have worked in this space for some time, whilst others work hard to maintain currency. Returning to Hordern's (2021) argument, this suggests some training provides are more attuned to FE sector practices than others. This matters, as Bound (2011) argues, as teachers' development needs to be contextualised to practices and their teaching environment, so not understanding this context is a disadvantage to the trainer and to those undertaking the development.

11.6 Methodology

Our methodology was to recognise the research-capable staff working within the RCG member organisations and use these skills to develop the skills of others 'neophyte' researchers within the sector. In recognition of these skills, we took the unusual step of renumerating all staff for the work they undertook, and this allowed staff to work in their own time overcoming two of the key barriers for the sectors practitioner-researchers: time and recognition. Member organisations identified staff who could contribute to a review of the literature and/or conduct, transcribe, and analyse a structured interview. In order to develop the capacity of those researchers with less experience, we ensured that training was offered and that less experienced researchers were paired with or supported by more experienced researchers.

To ensure that knowledge of practice was treated in parity with more theoretical or conceptual 'academic' work, we ensured that practice focused work published in sector facing spaces, such as the Educational and Training Foundation's Outstanding Teaching, Learning and Assessment, was included in terms of parity with 'academic' work published in journals, as does this chapter. The four members of the literature review team split into two groups to review these two forms of knowing the sector and created a spreadsheet which identified key recommendations for practice. Working in this way, we were able to conduct a thematic analysis (Braun and Clarke, 2006) to explore for areas of overlap and commonality between the two perspectives.

The research questions for this section were as follows:

RQ 1 Identify practical interventions that progress learners and improve outcomes for 16- to 19-year-olds in FE working towards achieving Level 2 in English.

RQ 2 Understand which interventions may develop learners' confidence in their understanding of the subjects, abilities in applying that understanding, and about taking exams.

In order to understand current practice alongside the published work, we created an interview team. Each interviewer undertook two interviews in a member organisation, one of a manager of GCSE English res-sits and one of a key practitioner in this area. Understanding the current state of practice was important and practice is continually developing (Hordern, 2021), and moreover the work took place post-covid, so proximity to the site of knowledge told us that lockdowns had had an impact on aspects of both learner and teacher behaviour which needed to be understood and included in the development. The interviews took place via Teams and were recorded and transcribed (see Figure 11.1 for a list of the interview questions). The interviewer then completed a findings summary document that recorded key themes and supporting quotations, and this was brought together by a team that analysed all interviewers' findings and triangulated against the findings from the review of the literature.

The main themes from the literature and practice reviews, along with the areas of overlap between them, were presented in the Venn diagram which is the

	Question
Q1	What are your roles and responsibilities within your organisation?
Q2	Tell me about the team that delivers English GCSE resits in you organisation.
Q3	What do you consider to be the most pressing issues surrounding English resit teaching in your organisation?
Q4	a. What do you feel are the biggest barriers for **staff** in your organisation to improving your GCSE English results? b. What teaching or curriculum interventions do you put in place to address these?
Q5	a. What do you feel are the biggest barriers for **students** studying for English resits? b. What teaching or curriculum interventions do you put in place to address these?
Q6	Can you tell me about a 'star' English teacher in your organisation and what makes them such a successful teacher? (Alternative, what do you feel makes a successful English teacher?)
Q7	What teaching or curriculum interventions have you put in place that have had the greatest success?
Q8	What internal or external support would benefit you and your team to improve GCSE English delivery?
Q9	What areas of the GCSE English resit syllabus would you (or your students) like to have more support or training. Be as specific as you like ...is it a particular topic or area?
Q10	What barriers would your staff face in accessing the support? How could they be overcome?

Figure 11.1 Interview questions

centre circle on the ThingLink in Figure 11.2. The work was presented in this manner to make the findings quickly visible to our clients, and practitioners and senior management teams within member organisations. This relates back to the RCG's aim to make the work 'useful', and to the discussion regarding the development of legitimate language and voice in the sector that is inclusive to all. Moreover, if further information was required, then the ThingLink allowed the reader to click through to see the data and analysis sitting behind the work.

As the RCG had created its own Ethics Committee and processes, ethics clearance for the project came from this source.

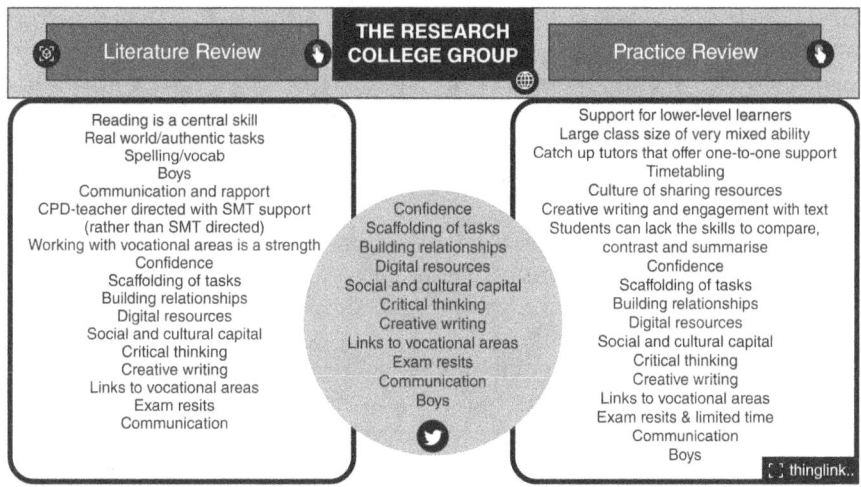

Figure 11.2 ThingLink: https://www.thinglink.com/card/1823677041539547622

11.7 Findings

In terms of the findings from the project, we can see from the centre of the Venn diagram above that the key themes included issues regarding the subject knowledge and skills around the subject, and social context of the learners. However, for the purpose of this chapter, this is not the focus.

What was interesting to us was where the exploration of current practice through the interviews gave fresh context to existing issues. We found that the persistent problems around confidence and communication in students taking GCSE English had been compounded by the recent Covid-19 lockdowns. This was not something present in the literature, but exploring the practice alongside it allowed us to add this valuable context to our findings.

At the end of the project, we were able to reflect on our ability to build the capacity from within the sector through our methodology of more and less experienced staff working together. In the main, this was a largely successful approach which included unexpected benefits. Bringing the practitioner researchers into contact with each other exposed sector staff to each other's publications and thoughts as well as identify isolated researchers from within organisations. This not only increased our understanding of the scope of work which was initially not visible to us but helps to create a community where practitioner researchers feel valued and a sense of belonging.

The findings of the project itself went to inform part of a Department for Education initiative to develop practice in GCSE resits. That in itself is a lot to unpack. The use of practitioner work informed the wider development of the sector's practice at the level of policy. This gave those practitioners an influence that, as I have discussed, is sadly missing from sector developments. Moreover, the work was produced by other researchers working within the sector. The sector was thinking, speaking, and acting entirely autonomously. Here, there was no one needed to speak for them or interpret and seek to understand them. The sector workers had done that work for themselves.

The dissemination at the level of policy and practice, I would argue, demonstrates the value of FE practitioner knowledge and research and gives concrete examples of where it can be successfully included with other forms of research and done so in terms of parity.

In terms of the wider aims of the RCG, this project makes a good argument for the inclusion of practitioner research into large projects as it can provide a context not achievable elsewhere. I also argue it demonstrates the value of FE practitioner knowledge and research and gives concrete examples of where it can be successfully included with other forms of research and done so in terms of parity.

I have discussed earlier that the barriers of time and recognition were addressed by the renumeration for the work. This was facilitated by the funding received for the work from the training provider, which meant that money aimed at understanding and developing the sector stayed *within* the sector to further develop capacity, rather than going outside to third parties.

The project as a whole modelled methodologies for using practitioner research in the development of the sector and in recognising its value in understanding the values and norms of practices. We see this work as early stages, and there have been issues with some of our decisions. For example, we have found the ThingLink not to be a very stable platform in terms of the stability and accessibility of the links, and the standard of presentation in some elements of the work has not always been the standard we would have liked. But we would argue that this is overshadowed by achievement of using, developing, and creating a value for the practitioner research included in the sector-led project, which is unlike so many others that are led by, or explore from, the outside the sector. Both have their value, but at present one has the higher status.

11.8 Conclusions

My conclusions are that there is a place for practitioner research in the development of the sector. It creates a contextual and practice-focused complement to other forms of research. From this standpoint, it would appear that the lack of use of practitioner knowledge is more closely aligned with its lack of status than its lack of 'usefulness'.

The work also shows that the sector has the skills and abilities to lead large research projects itself if barriers are addressed. It demonstrates that there is a pool of opportunity and talent within the sector; the question remains, however, the degree to which the sector itself wishes to recognise, remunerate, and normalise this work.

References

Appleby, Y. and Hillier, Y. (2012) 'Exploring practice – research networks for professional learning', *Studies in Continuing Education*, 34(1), pp. 31–43.

Atkins, L. and Tummons, J. (2017) 'Professionalism in vocational education: international perspectives', *Research in Post-Compulsory Education*, 22(3), pp. 355–369.

Bernstein, B. (2000). *Pedagogy, symbolic control, and identity: theory, research, critique*. Vol. 5. Oxford: Rowman & Littlefield.

Bound, H. (2011) 'Vocational education and training teacher professional development: tensions and context', *Studies in Continuing Education*, 33(2), pp. 107–119.

Braun, V. and Clarke, V. (2006) 'Using thematic analysis in psychology', *Qualitative Research in Psychology*, 3(2), pp. 77–101.

Chen, J., Derrick, J., Duncan, S., Hayward, G., Jones, S. and Smith, L. (2025) 'Doing research or being researched? Debates on 'Close-to-Practice' research from the perspective of the further, adult and vocational education (FAVE) sector', in Wyse, B., Baumfield, V., Mockler, N. and Reardon, M. (eds.) *The BERA-SAGE international handbook of research-informed education policy and practice*. London: SAGE.

Elliott, G. (1996) 'Why is research invisible in further education?', *British Educational Research Journal*, 22(1), pp. 101–111.

Gregson, M. (2020) 'In practice: the importance of practitioner research in vocational education', *Education Sciences*, 10(3), p. 79.

Hordern, J. (2021) 'Why close to practice is not enough: neglecting practice in educational research', *British Educational Research Journal*, 47(6), pp. 1451–1465.

Lloyd, C. and Jones, S. (2018) 'Researching the sector from within: the experience of establishing a research group within an FE college', *Research in Post-Compulsory Education*, 23(1), pp. 75–93.

Martell, C.C., Carney, M.M., Marin, K.A. and Hashimoto-Martell, E.A. (2021) 'Whose research counts? Teacher research and the practitioner-academic divide', *The Teacher Educator*, 56(4), pp. 399–426.

McNiff, J., Lomax, P. and Whitehead, J. (2003) *You and your action research project*. Abingdon: Routledge.

Richardson, K., Lloyd, C. and Donovan, C. (2023) Towards a democratic professionalism in further education: building from the 'ground-up', *Management in Education*. https://doi.org/10.1177/08920206231187344.

Part IV

Stories of leadership

Chapter 12

Unblocking the FE leadership pipeline

Understanding today's senior leaders in order to inspire tomorrow's

Rebecca Gater

12.1 Introduction

This chapter is based on an original thesis, submitted in part fulfilment of a Doctorate in Education (EdD) with Liverpool Hope University. 'Five Lives and I: Exploring Further Education Senior Leaders' identities through life history' (Gater, 2022) is available via ResearchGate: https://www.researchgate.net/publication/363311562_Five_lives_and_I_exploring_further_education_senior_leaders%27_identities_through_life_history.

One of the first challenges I faced when I started my EdD was an assessed presentation about professional context, identity and values. As part of that, I had to reflect on my professional identity and values. Whilst I felt confident about my professional values, I struggled to think critically about my career trajectory and why I moved from teaching into a leadership role. I could not articulate how and why I came to be in the role I was in (at that time, Assistant Principal in a Further Education (FE) college), and neither could I confidently describe my professional identity. At that point, I felt intrigued as to whether others in my position felt the same, or whether they could justify and articulate their professional identity and the choices they had made in their careers to date. Therefore, it made sense to me to focus my research on exploring the professional identities of senior leaders in FE, particularly on those whose career trajectories have taken them from teaching into leadership roles. The research delves into the significant moments in individuals' lives that have led them to move from teaching into leadership. Whilst this research contributes to knowledge on FE senior leaders, it has also supported me to 'make sense of my own story and experiences' (Weston, 2015, p. 4).

By researching the stories of senior leaders in FE, and gaining a better understanding of who they are, I am keen to 'shine a light' on senior leadership, to encourage others to pursue these roles in the future as viable and desirable career options. Or in other words, to highlight the origins of today's senior leaders, in order to inspire tomorrow's.

12.2 Research questions, aims and objectives

The aim of my research was to explore the life histories of current FE senior leaders, by investigating the reasons for teachers moving into senior leadership careers in FE, establishing what type of leader they are, and exploring the factors that have shaped this. Professional identities of senior leaders is an under-researched area, as is leadership in FE; much current research in FE focuses on middle managers, and professional identities of teachers. I am hopeful that by researching and sharing the stories of senior leaders in FE, others will be given the confidence to pursue a leadership career of their own, which will ultimately prevent the looming leadership crisis.

The overarching research question underpinning my research is as follows:

To what extent does life history impact on teachers moving into senior leadership positions in FE?

To address the overarching question, the following research questions (RQ) were formulated:

RQ 1 – *How do senior leaders define their identities?*

RQ 2 – *How have the life experiences of senior leaders in FE influenced their career paths?*

RQ 3 – *What/which critical incidents/moments/events contributed to individuals' decisions to take on senior leadership roles?*

RQ 4 – *How have their leadership style, behaviours and professional identity/ies been shaped?*

12.3 Positionality

As a senior leader in FE, I felt that it was important to position myself throughout my research as the interviewer, the researcher and the researched. I was interested in how my participants' lives had shaped their journeys to senior leadership, but I also wanted this research to provide me with some clarity about my own identity as an FE senior leader. In order to make sense of my life experiences and how they have impacted my professional career, I wanted to compare my life experiences with my participants' by writing myself into the research (Goodson and Sikes, 2018). Reflecting on my life during the research process was as cathartic as it was illuminating; bringing to light how critical events or moments have shaped particular characteristics which have been instrumental in my career trajectory.

This perspective very much positioned me as an 'insider' insofar as I am a senior leader in FE, and therefore shared with my participants a role and a type of workplace. Drake and Heath (2011) state that 'insiders often have assumptions and ideas about what they expect to find out' and as they are practitioners they also 'often have a theoretical stance before beginning' their research (p. 20). I must confess that I was guilty of this to some extent; considering my own experience and professional identity and picking up informally on the life experiences of others in my field, I had certain assumptions about the type of critical events and moments that may have impacted on my participants' desire to pursue leadership roles. However, I was not so wedded to these assumptions that I was not objective enough to listen to, and analyse, the perceptions of those participating in my study.

12.4 Existing knowledge

The key topics pertinent to the aims and research questions for this study are leadership and management in FE, and professional identity.

12.4.1 FE leadership and management

Existing research suggests that breaking down barriers created by hierarchical structures and creating an ethos of togetherness and teamwork is where leadership is at its finest. This professional approach to leadership and management is the key driver to organisational improvement and success and forms strong values through building colleagues' trust, being an 'authentic' leader, role modelling high standards, consistently demonstrating shared values and beliefs and being transparent. As Jupp (2015) claims, 'Leadership is both determined by and shapes the culture and context of a college' (p. 178).

However, at the time of incorporation in 1992, management within the private sector was believed to be superior and more effective than that within the public sector. It was therefore deemed necessary for senior leaders in FE colleges to focus on 'the golden three E's' – economy, efficiency and effectiveness (Randle and Brady, 1997, p. 125). This style of management caused controversy and conflict, with more strike days in FE colleges at that time than in any other public sector organisation (Smithers and Robinson, 2000). Thankfully, at the turn of the 21st century, the top-down styles of management were replaced by a more affiliative and co-operative style of management which emphasised a shared purpose within organisations. During this period of time, there was an influx of female managers, which some believe supported a more feminised approach to management. Leaders nowadays are increasingly aware and conscious of the impact that their style has on staff motivation and morale. Current training programmes, such as the Association of Colleges' (AoC) 'senior leadership development programme', 'leading from the middle' and the ETF's 'Preparing for CEO' are designed to support managers to be better skilled and able to interpret business requirements, making them meaningful to colleagues. The most effective leaders today generally bond and engage with staff to pursue common goals and values, creating a followership rather than demonstrating superiority and self-importance. This approach to consciously engage and motivate colleagues is more prominent in the modern-day college and is the key driver to organisational improvement and success.

12.4.2 Professional identity

Identity can loosely be described as the ongoing effort to answer the questions 'who am I?' and 'how should I act?' (Lundberg, 2019). There is a school of thought that identity can be simply boiled down to a set of individual's traits, competencies and values (Alvesson, 2010). However, there are other theories that individuals build their identity upon life experiences, culture and environment starting from early childhood until the present day (McAdams, 1996). It could be argued, however, that both theories are accurate; ongoing throughout individuals' lives, the experiences shape the values and vice versa.

Lundberg (2019) suggests that leaders constantly evaluate, negotiate, calibrate and redefine their identity through a series of 'leadership moments' (p. 212), and these moments are critical in terms of defining and validating leadership identity. A comprehensive collection of leadership moments is built over time, and as experience grows, give leaders a diverse range of experiences to draw upon to deal with a variety of tasks and activities. This facilitates a constant and intuitive construction of the individual's leadership identity.

Existing research in FE senior leadership suggests that role models, and equally those displaying poor examples of leadership, have an impact on senior leaders and how they interact with their colleagues. For example, where individuals have admired leaders, they tend to emulate their behaviours, attitudes and values in their own practice. However, those that have experienced a poor leadership style have learned how not to behave, in order to get the best results from their teams. Learning from these role models, good and bad, has helped to inform both professional practice and leadership identity.

12.4.3 The existing context

I included five participants in my research in addition to myself. All my participants were practising senior leaders in English FE colleges who started life in the sector as teachers. Due to new working protocols in Covid-19, I was able to conduct my research interviews online via MS Teams or Zoom, so was able to draw upon a diverse geographical range that I would not have managed to do in person, for example as far North as Newcastle, and as far South as Bournemouth, with others in between.

12.5 Methodology

I had clear criteria for selecting my participants – they had to be practicing senior leaders in an English FE college, and they had to have progressed to a senior leadership role following a teaching career. I used my professional networks such as LinkedIn to 'advertise' for participants and asked those in my networks to share far and wide.

Each participant was interviewed at least twice, adopting a hybrid model combining Wengraf's (2016) biographical-narrative-interpretive model and a life chapters tool (McAdams et al., 2018).

12.6 Hybrid approach to life history interviews

Figure 12.1 illustrated data analysis running in parallel with data collection as I saw both as two halves of the same whole. I created a four-stage data analysis process (see Figure 12.2), combining a range of techniques which continually review the data and reflect on it, ensuring that analysis is ongoing and iterative (Goodson and Sikes, 2018). This collection of data analysis illuminated and gave life to the narratives, supporting me to form early findings to be built upon and strengthened with each participant. I was very careful not to enter the research with a clear hypothesis; preferring to interview the participants in a very open-minded manner, letting their data tell its own story.

In order to protect my participants, they were offered the opportunity to select a pseudonym to ensure anonymity and confidentiality, and those not wishing to select their own were offered a range of alternatives to choose from. All participants consented to me using the video recording function to record the interviews. Participants had a right to withdraw themselves and their data at any time during the research process, and this was made clear to them throughout.

Stage 1	Interview 1 – Part 1 A single question designed to induce narrative (Wengraf, 2016); I combined this with the life chapters approach (McAdams, 2018), asking participants to think of their life in chapters and tell me about those chapters in any order they felt comfortable with. A short break, including light refreshments and some fresh air, followed.
Stage 2	Interview 1 – Part 2 A reflection on the key words, phrases and critical moments as told by the participants, followed by questions to probe further into their narrative.
Stage 3	In between interviews I listened back to the audio-recordings and conducted some initial analysis of key language, phrases, events, thoughts and emotions and noted some specific questions surrounding these.
Stage 4	Interview 2 A loose framework of topics from my reflections provided me with questions designed to give more context and understanding to the individuals' narrative.

Figure 12.1 Data collection and analysis stages

Stage 1	• Listen to and watch the interview repeatedly, noting any pertinent non-verbal cues such as body language, intonation, pauses etc • Write summaries which notes what has been said, key words and phrases, verbatim quotations and short extracts
Stage 2	• Listen to and watch the interview repeatedly • Read summary notes repeatedly • Write a thorough and detailed profile on the life of each participant. Sample in appendix one
Stage 3	• Draw a map (I used software called 'coggle.it') to pictorially evidence commonalities and differences in life history and experiences – which supported me to identify themes • The maps are designed to highlight key events, critical moments and trigger points in individual's lives.
Stage 4	• Analyse and decide on the key themes – create thematic maps including data on the theme from each participant, including myself. Example in appendix two

Figure 12.2 Four stage data analysis process (Gater, 2022)

12.7 Findings

RQ 1 – *How do senior leaders define their identities?*

The key demographic and value-based factors which when combined influence the participants' personal and professional identity are as follows:

- Age – Though age is inconsequential for most participants, those who mentioned it were in their 50s and did so from a future career planning perspective.
- Gender – In the past, research identified an under-representation of female senior leaders in FE. However, AoC (2021) data demonstrates that this is no longer the case – 55% of college leaders are female. Female participants saw their gender as unimportant, as they did not need to break through the 'glass ceiling' to reach senior leadership posts as others have before them
- Race – All but one of the participants are White British, and their Whiteness was 'defined through exclusion' (Liu and Baker, 2016, p. 424). Those who mentioned their race did so to explain situations in which they were in a minority, for example when visiting other (typically non-White-British) countries, though interestingly their race afforded them advantages rather than disadvantages. Their experiences are converse when compared to the experiences of ethnically diverse leaders who have experienced barriers to career progression due to their race (Johnson, 2017). Whilst Morrissey's (2015) research suggests that 'difference equals deficit' (p. 228), it seems

that this applies to ethnically diverse individuals when they are in the minority, but not necessarily for White individuals when they have experienced being a minority.
- Perceived social class – All but one of the participants perceive themselves to have come from a 'working-class' background, though none referred to their current status. As most participants come from working-class backgrounds and now find themselves in what could be perceived to be traditionally middle-class careers, this suggests that social mobility is strengthening in the 21st century, within the field of education, increasing middle-class and decreasing working-class populations (Evans and Mellon, 2016).
- The senior leaders' professional identity is built around: being authentic – they show a great deal of concern and awareness of how their leadership impacts on others; being a 'people person' – sharing an overwhelming desire to value people and invest in professional relationships; being a 'jack of all trades' – due to increasing areas of responsibility as they were employed in more senior posts, participants recognised that they were no longer experts in their area, as they had been in junior or middle management positions; being strategic, responsible and accountable – there is a strong recognition that being a senior leader brings a great deal of accountability, and 'the buck stops with you'.
- The senior leaders' personal identity is built upon family – with many participants moving to FE after having children, starting part time and building up their hours as the children grew; and maintaining a work-life balance – valuing social activities and spending quality and relaxing time with friends and family.
- Motivation and values are common, with participants being motivated by making a difference to others, being ambitious and having an intrinsic desire to push themselves, maximising earning potential due to having a family, and wanting to become a Principal/CEO.

RQ 2 – *How have the life experiences of senior leaders in FE influenced their career paths?*

12.7.1 Family background

Coming from working-class backgrounds has afforded most of these senior leaders an element of choice and flexibility, as they were not under pressure from their families to go to university or enter a professional career.

12.7.2 Education

Though they did not necessarily have a formulated career plan at the age of 16, all participants went on to study and successfully achieve level 3 qualifications, whether A levels or vocational qualifications. All but one went to university, mostly the first in their family, and the majority emigrated within the UK, crossing their home county border for study. Since then, all participants have achieved Degree level qualifications, four have achieved Master's degrees, and I now hold a Doctorate.

12.7.3 Work

Most senior leaders in this study entered FE as hourly paid lecturers after having careers in other industries and for most, this decision was taken after having children. Previous teaching experience was not essential; though some had experienced teaching in the community, or in a higher education institution, an equal number had no previous experience at all. Two participants and I had worked in management roles before entering FE, but for the remainder, managing the department they had previously been part of was their first experience of management, despite teaching and management requiring different skills and no formal training being provided in preparation.

RQ 3 – *What/which critical incidents/moments/events contributed to individuals' decisions to take on senior leadership roles?*

12.7.4 Opportunities

The senior leaders were presented with opportunities which they subsequently optimised towards their success; commonly making a sideways move following a period of dissatisfaction, relocation or voluntary redundancy which were risky decisions to make but paid off in terms of career trajectory and entering senior leadership.

12.7.5 Restructures

All senior leaders in this study experienced at least one, if not multiple, restructures. For this group, the restructures, though stressful at the time, have proved advantageous catalysts for change, securing senior leadership positions often with more influence.

12.7.6 Dysfunction

It is unfortunate that all participants experienced dysfunction at work to the degree that they sought alternative employment. The causes and symptoms of the dysfunction varied, but most commonly were due to poor leadership which resulted in an unpleasant culture.

RQ4 – *How have their leadership style, behaviours and professional identity/ies been shaped?*

The participants' notion of leadership, and how they successfully enact strong and effective leadership, is centred around the concepts of collaboration, consultation, empowerment, building relationships, empathy, openness and transparency. In many cases, the senior leaders had a great deal of self-awareness regarding how they, and their leadership, were perceived by others due to their own experiences of poor leadership in the past; for example, disempowering and undervaluing others too much 'stick' and not enough 'carrot'. Those who held leadership positions previously developed transferrable leadership skills which they have brought with them into FE, such as staff development, gaining feedback to improve practice and recognising and praising good performance.

Learning from role models has also been an important factor in shaping senior leaders' leadership style and behaviours, particularly when they are exposed early career.

12.8 Conclusion

Despite contextual nuances, all five participants and I have experienced very similar life histories and share similar attitudes, values, motivations and ambitions. Findings from the life history interviews confirm that all of the senior leader participants are 'ordinary' people: they have not led privileged lives that others may perceive them to have lived, and they do not have any 'superpowers' that are not attainable by others aspiring to become senior leaders in the future. Despite this, the FE leadership pipeline remains blocked; the metaphors used by the media to describe the sector present a senior leader population of old, White men, with women struggling to break through glass ceilings, therefore constraining the narrative (Gater, 2021), deterring ambitious middle managers from seeking these positions as they do not identify with the narrative. The narrative needs serious updating and FE leadership needs re-humanising and re-energising to remove the pipeline blockage and stop the potential crisis, making way for ambitious and inspired senior leaders to enter the fold.

References

Alvesson, M. (2010) 'Self-doubters, strugglers, storytellers, surfers and others: images of selfidentities in organization studies', *Human Relations*, 63(2), pp. 193–217.
Association of Colleges. (2021) College key facts 2021–22. https://www.aoc.co.uk/about/college-key-facts [Accessed 3 October 2022].
Bailey-morrissey, C. (2015) *An exploration of the lived experiences of Black women secondary school leaders*. London, UK: University of Roehampton/Kingston University.

Drake, P. and Heath, L. (2011) *Practitioner research at doctoral level: developing coherent research methodologies.* Oxon: Routledge.

Evans, G. and Mellon, J. (2016) 'Social class: identity, awareness and political attitudes: why are we still working class?', *British Social Attitudes*, 33. https://www.bsa.natcen.ac.uk/latest-report/british-social-attitudes-33/introduction.aspx [Accessed: 3 October 2022].

Gater, R. (2021) 'Gender in education', in *Association for Research in Post Compulsory Education. Social Justice seminar series.*

Gater, R. (2022). 'Five lives and I: exploring further education senior leaders' identities through life history'. Thesis for Doctorate of Education. Birmingham, UK: Birmingham Newman University. doi: 10.13140/RG.2.2.21543.83361.

Goodson, I. and Sikes, P. (2018) 'Techniques for doing life history', in Goodson, I. et al. (eds.) *The Routledge international handbook on narrative and life history.* London: Routledge, pp. 72–88.

Johnson, L. (2017) 'The lives and identities of UK Black and South Asian head teachers: metaphors of leadership', *Educational Management Administration and Leadership*, 45(5), pp. 842–862.

Jupp, T. (2015) 'Leadership and leaders of colleges', in Hodgson, A. (ed.) *Coming of age for FE?: reflections on the past and future role for further education colleges in England.* London, UK: Institute of Education Press, pp. 178–198.

Liu, H. and Baker, C. (2016) 'White Knights: leadership as the heroicisation of whiteness', *Leadership*, 12(4), pp. 420–448.

Lundberg, M. (2019) *Trust and self-trust in leadership identity constructions: a qualitative exploration of narrative ecology in the discursive aftermath of heroic discourse.* PhD thesis. Copenhagen, Denmark: Copenhagen Business School.

McAdams, D. (1996) 'Personality, modernity, and the storied self: a contemporary framework for studying persons', *Psychological Inquiry*, 7, pp. 295–321.

McAdams, D. (2018) 'How stories found a home in human personality', in Goodson, I. et al. (eds.) *The Routledge international handbook on narrative and life history.* London, UK: Routledge, pp. 34–49.

Randle, K. and Brady, N. (1997) 'Managerialism and professionalism in the 'cinderella service'', *Journal of Vocational Education and Training*, 49(1), pp. 121–139.

Smithers, A. and Robinson, P. (2000) *Coping with teacher shortages.* London: National Union of Teachers.

Wengraf, T. (2016) *Qualitative research interviewing, qualitative research interviewing.* London: Sage Publications.

Weston, J. (2015) *Passion, pragmatics and politics – senior women leaders in further education: an exploration of leadership style and identity.* EdD thesis. Bristol, UK: University of the West of England.

Appendix

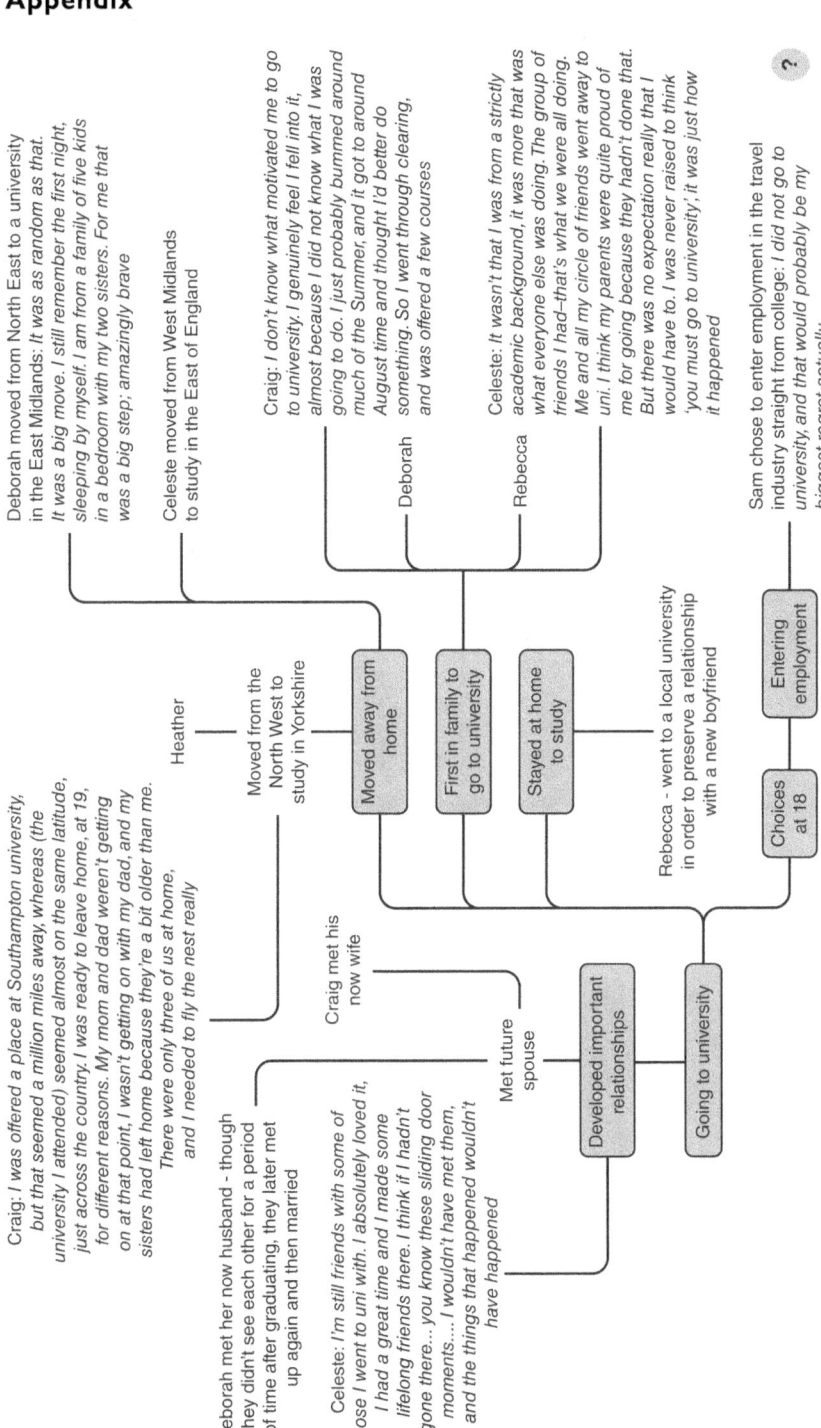

Figure A.1 Post-18 education section of life history map (Source: Gater, 2022)

> Whilst in that role, Craig encountered a Deputy Principal, who 'became a really good mentor', and 'took me under his wing'. Craig learned a lot from him, particularly around looking at things from a broader perspective, and that one can be effective and efficient within 'normal working hours' rather than being the first in the office and the last out. 'I was young and naive, and he helped to guide me.' Craig stayed in that role for just over five years,
>
>> *'I think being so young, becoming a manager of quite a number of people, by the time I'd done 5 years there of doing that kind of thing, I already felt pretty comfortable as a manager. I just learned on the job. I remember, it feels like a long time ago, my exams officer going off sick, everything was in danger of coming crashing down. Having to deal with that sort of stuff, you know, student services, all stuff I'd never done before. And very quickly I had to move away from the more technical stuff and just become a more general manager.'*
>>
>> Researcher: *'So why do you think that you were the last man standing so to speak?'*
>>
>> Craig: *'This is not blowing my own trumpet; this is more luck than judgement. I w3sa looking after [named two departments] which were high profile, and [they] didn't have any friends who worked in those areas so [they] couldn't replace me like the others.'*
>
> Around two years into his tenure, the area review suggested a merge with a local college which was successfully accomplished, validated by a positive Ofsted inspection.
>
> Thinking about the transference of leadership attributes from work to home, Craig confirms that he does make most big family decisions, but in day-to-day life, 'my kids are amazed I've got this job. They think I'm stupid and completely immature, which I probably am at home!'

Figure A.2 Extract from Craig's profile (Source: Gater, 2022)

Conclusion

Sam Jones and Kerry Scattergood

This chapter explores themes from throughout the book, including professional identity, how we know what we know, culture and capacity and restraints on the sector. There were many other themes that occurred to us as we edited the book, but sadly there were too many to include here. We hope you, the reader, as well as enjoying specific chapters that you can relate to your own work, have picked up on themes that interest you from across the chapters. We have tried to encapsulate the main ideas from each chapter in this concluding chapter, but we are conscious that much remains unsaid. We hope this book, therefore, offers the beginning of a conversation for some readers, thinking about themes such as leadership, professionalism, collaboration, shaping pedagogy and being aware of the things that frustrate these (to coin Patrick and Christine), such as performativity/managerial issues which have challenged some of our authors. That said, there is much richness to unpack under the four themes we have identified. In order to add our own voices to this conversation, we also offer one possible view for the future of practitioner research in the sector.

Professional identity

Several of the chapters explore concepts of professional identity within practitioner research. As we explore these chapters, we acknowledge the importance of practitioner choice and agency, which reoccurs throughout most chapters. For Francine Warren, it is important to allow teachers to develop their own agency, especially in being brave to take risks in their own practice. For Catherine Lloyd, participants make choices based on their values about which forms of knowledge to draw on when making pedagogical decisions. For Kerry Scattergood, the opportunity to research her own practice not only gives her choice and agency but also enables the agency of the participants to shape their identity around their writing. For Chloë Hynes, it comes from selecting what is professionally important. For Bryony Evett Hackfort, it is important teachers have choice not only over what they research but also over the whole process, from methodology to decisions regarding how to share their work. This illustrates that there is a wide conceptualisation of choice and agency running through the work, much of the work seems to not only develop the identity of the researcher but also facilitate the development of the identity of those around them. This suggests that although 25 years ago Avis (1999) argued that the research culture in Further Education (FE) was being used to performative and financial measures that still persist in the sector, the forms of practitioner work we are seeing now are perhaps a little more focused on highlighting the gaps in which 'to dance' (Daley, Orr and Petrie, 2015), to think and to develop.

Throughout the chapters, our authors articulate not only how research helps them position who they are, but also who they are not. Considering who we are, Kerry Scattergood and Fey Cole perceive research as an opportunity to understand who they both are. Sam Jones, and Patrick O'Donnell and Christine Calder are recognising practitioner-researchers as researchers, and this should be acknowledged as part of their role within a college. Clare Sutton highlights the tension in the competing identities of course leaders in college-based higher education, feeling invisible which led her to research. Looking at who we are not, Catherine Lloyd takes a stance on the insider/outsider debate, whereby professional identity is about understanding who you are when you are researching the practice of others within the sector. Katie Barrett declares she is not a researcher, but clearly the practice of research has transformed her day-to-day role. This suggests that the practitioner-researchers are working with some complex and sometimes competing identities. This underlies the challenges of finding the gaps to dance within the sector and speaks to the difficulties of feeling like a 'legitimate' researcher. At the same time, Katie's chapter points to the benefits to the individual teacher of undertaking this sometimes challenging work.

How do we know what we know?

According to Pring (2007, p. 155), for Dewey truth lies 'in warranted guidance for future action'. By this he is arguing that knowledge is belief tied to some form of evidence that makes it true. In much of the work, the warrant is the seen in the successful application to practice. Therefore, most of the chapters in this book can be argued to develop knowledge through action and activities. The researchers set goals for their activities, seek to understand the conditions around the activities and draw on their experience and knowledge to syllogise, or make decisions, take action and then evaluate against the intended aims. For example, Rachel Arnold aims to engage her GCSE re-sit students by changing position with them, allowing the students become the experts and teachers become the learners. She has used her professional judgement to decide the correct lever to make the change is to build student-relationships, and by connecting with the students, closes the empathy gap. She then measures and evaluates the initiative, creating new conceptual perspectives, as well as practice developments, on the problem. When considering the Research College Group (RCG), Sam Jones argues that it is the understanding of the norms of the practice that positions practitioner research as separate from other forms of knowing. Knowing practice, and being in practice, researchers know which levers to pull, how to mould it, how to change it and how you can improve it.

Chloë Hynes knew there was a problem as it could be seen in the classroom and, for her, research was an opportunity to solve that problem. There was a tension between policy and practice, and she was able to resolve the tension and engage her students. This was achieved by drawing on her own experience, those of other teachers around her practice and by drawing on theory. We see her reading Phil Race, and also seeking to understand the needs of the students she, and others, are teaching. She brings together this knowledge and tests her work to create her warrant. She develops what looks initially like new paperwork. But scratch beneath that surface and new practices and pedagogies are introduced via the paperwork. These are the practices and pedagogies that, in Chloë's professional judgement, meet the needs of the learners and goals that are facing her and when these are introduced into practice, she evaluates their impact on the students.

Sometimes coming to 'know' isn't a comfortable experience. For example, Clare chose to research the thorny issues around time that were dogging her practice, and whilst she came to understand the context and the reasoning for the position she found herself in, she wasn't able to change it. This is an important limitation for all types of research, not just those undertaken by practitioners. There will be issues that will be too large for one person to move or address, but this is not to say these should not be researched as indeed understanding these more fully facilitates understanding what an eventual solution may be.

Culture and capacity

When looking at creating models for practitioner research, role-modelling and capacity-building are important mechanisms. Both Fey Cole and Sam Jones discuss the importance of role-modelling. Whilst Fey role-models the expectations or values that she asks of others as their manager, Sam notes the RCG uses it as a method of capacity development by having a more-experienced researcher and less-experienced researcher working together, with the more-experienced researcher role-modelling values and practices. Bryony Evett Hackfort is raising capacity by recognising action research as legitimate continuous professional development by developing the thinking and skills and embedding it into the organisation through a 'culture of curiosity'.

While the three chapters discussed above consider culture and capacity at an organisational, or multiple organisational level, Francine Warren, Rachel Arnold and Kerry Scattergood are looking at capacity-development at an individual level. For both Rachel and Kerry, their initial research has been a starting point for further research and capacity development when studying for their doctorates. Francine, through developing her personal understanding, is developing the practices and values of future generations of teachers.

The examples discussed in this section point to a capacity *within* the sector that can develop both the individuals and organisations within it. This suggests to us that the sector is capable of developing its own research culture and capacity, and indeed some of the mechanisms to do so, such as role-modelling and value development, as well as the points of exchange and storage of work that have been explored in the 'context of the sector' chapter are in place to do so.

Restraints on sector

When looking at restraints on researchers within the sector, Patrick O'Donnell and Christine Calder explore what frustrates research in the sector, including the current priorities and operational pressures. The difficulties of researching and making that work visible have been explored well by Elliott (1996) and more recently by Chen et al. (2025). The good news for anyone reading this book is that despite these frustrations, the work in this area appears to be developing. Organisational pressures are seen in the work of Clare Sutton and Katie Barrett, where both researchers and participants struggle with time and workload. Again, these chapters point to the difference in the size of the structural issues being the deciding factor, meaning that the practitioner researcher may possess sufficient agency to work with others to overcome them, as in the case of Katie and her nurses' managers, or that the issue is just too large and fundamental to the sector to move, in the case of Clare. For Catherine Lloyd and Chloë Hynes, the macro and micro policy issues that surround the work and the work of their participants are the overarching restraining issues. Catherine's agriculture teachers are adapting practices around industrial and environmental pressures, really reflecting an ability to make pedagogical decisions in a complex environment, whereas Chloë's constraints are the type of local policies that sometimes require adaption to work in a particular context.

Again, this suggests a variety of constraints facing practitioner researchers in the sector, which can sometimes be the grit in the oyster of new practice and developments, but can also simply be a shackle to those working in the sector. What is positive is the research work continues and so does what is known about the sector and that many staff are able to find the agency to work in this space.

Debates, challenges and joys of developing the practitioner-researcher space in the Further Education sector

The chapters within this book open the door to some useful debates and helpful ideas about what practitioner research in the FE sector could look like. Here, we aim to open up questions about the development of work in this space that arise from our author's contributions, rather than offering our own opinions on which paths should be taken.

The first debate is around leadership of the work: should it be the top down or bottom up and does this matter? We can see successful models for both approaches. Bryony Evett-Hackfort has created successful culture to being together practice and research in her organisation from a senior role, similarly so has Fey. However, other models, such as the FEResearchmeet tend to take the bottom-up approach.

Whilst the bottom-up approach can be argued to be a more democratic and perhaps practitioner-led environment which encourages innovation and empowers practitioners to own and drive practice, it is not without its disadvantages. Models such as this place the burden of the activity on the individuals leading it and often this activity can remain both unrecognised and unappreciated or renumerated. These models run the risk of following the model that Clare discusses in her chapter with regard to the Higher Education Course Leaders role, which is additional work for no extra benefit other than professional pride. We would argue this is a model that does not work longer term in the interests of an individual's well-being.

That is not to underestimate the challenges of a top-down approach. This method of leading practice may risk the inherent problem of positional power and the work being led by someone who is not a practitioner and so understands less about it. Simply tacking 'and research' onto the job title of a senior leader's role is unlikely to get the engagement, development and thought that is still required to move forward practice, methodology and theorisation in the space that Sam argues for. Moreover, this approach risks the work becoming performative, to solely meet the agenda of an organisation, rather than exploring developments and shaping a better future. There is every chance that this approach will alienate the agentic, engaged practitioners undertaking the work and far from building the sense of community belonging that Fey discusses, the work becomes just another additional thing expected of an already heavily workloaded sector (see Clare's chapter).

But who leads the work is not the only area of contention. Within this debate is the recognition of those undertaking the research work. The chapters written by Kerry, Chloe, Rachel, Katie and Francine really highlight the degree to which research work can change an individual. If the sector is serious about developing a research culture, then there needs to be some forward thinking about what the sector will do with these people, how they and their knowledge can be put to best use and how this will be recognised and their contribution acknowledged.

Within this text, three of the authors have very reluctantly left FE for Higher Education settings, and they are just three in a long line of people making this move. If FE were Great Britain, this would be considered to be a brain drain, as resource moves elsewhere. This book has shown, as other have before it (see Lloyd and Jones, 2018), that becoming a researcher involves a shift in identity, and unless colleges and other organisations in the sector have a plan in place for harnessing this shift, it seems likely that this brain drain will continue, we would argue to the detriment of the sector.

The fact that the sector has the ability to lead itself is evident from Patrick and Christine's chapter, as well Bryony's, Fey's and Sam's. 'Leadership from within' is a key message. However, what that leadership could look like appears to be an interesting site for future developments.

What we learn from the chapters is that time is an issue across the sector (seen in Clare, Katie and Sam's chapters), but the work of the RCG demonstrates that there are levers or mechanisms through which to renumerate and reward, which is certainly one method for acknowledging or recognising staff that contribute and work in this space.

Another reward seems to be the 'use' of the work. If we look at Chloe's work as well as Fey's, Rachel's, Francine's, Katie's, Clare's and Kerry's, they are all about problem solving. As professionals, they exercise their judgement to address an issue. Therefore, if we look at recognition, then an organisation putting this work to use within their policies and practices appears to be another method of acknowledgement and recognition. That said, unless published in an academic journal, there is presently an issue for how to credit work and practices developed in the sector. It seems important that if an individual's work is moved into another space, then this is giving the same recognition as it would be if you were to reference a book or a published paper. This points to another developmental challenge for the sector.

As well as the problem-solving aspect of the work, there are also chapters that seek to explore and illustrate the complexity of thinking and its development. Here, the chapters from Catherine, Francine and Bryony are useful. Catherine's chapter really illustrates the types of knowledges that the agriculture lecturers pull together in order to make pedagogical decisions. These are complex and perhaps only fully visible to those working in the context. This points to the final debate. Does FE research need to look different to encompass the different knowledges in the sector, and the sometimes different purposes? In the same way that Catherine's lecturers have to value a range of knowledge from policy, to hand skills, environmental conditions and pedagogical constraint and hold them as equal, does research in the sector need to reflect this position? Do we need to argue that beautifully conceptualised work such as the post-doctoral, doctoral and master's work should be held in parity with work that holds its warrant in its application to practice, and do we need to theorise and develop methodologies in order to do this? Sam's chapter suggests we do, whereas others, such as Patrick and Christine's, point to a different perspective.

Chapter summary

We hope this conclusion illustrates the benefits, challenges and exhilaration that FE sector workers experience when working in this space.

Not only do these projects demonstrate the challenges faced by and the opportunities the authors have taken and created for raising capacity for research in the sector, but they also offer opportunities for you, the reader, to do the same. Whether you are inspired to create pedagogical conversations opportunities like Francine Warren; to try Teach the Teacher with your students like Rachel Arnold; whether you wish to create your own 'culture of curiosity' like Bryony Evett Hackfort; or maybe your college has a research ethos that makes you feel you'd be a good fit to join the RCG. There are opportunities within these pages to continue to raise the capacity for research of the sector, and we hope to see more publications such as this one, sharing and showcasing the breadth of research from all corners of FE: from colleges and sixth forms, work-based learning and offender learning, to adult and community learning and college-based higher education.

We began this book stating that it is a book about space, voice, ownership, professionalism and utility. We hope it encourages you to join and develop the spaces and practices we have explored, to consider your voice as valuable and to work out how you could add value to your setting. We hope more than anything that a book like this helps you to find your own your voice and professionalism as this is not something anyone can give you, but if it is not exercised, it is something that can be taken away.

References

Avis, J. (1999) 'Shifting identity: new conditions and the transformation of practice – teaching within post-compulsory education', *Journal of Vocational Education and Training*, 51(2), pp. 245–264. doi: 10.1080/13636829900200081

Chen, J., Derrick, J., Duncan, S., Hayward, G., Jones, S. and Smith, L. (2025) 'Doing research or being researched? Debates on 'Close-to-Practice' research from the perspective of the Further, Adult and Vocational Education (FAVE) sector', in Wyse, B., Baumfield, V., Mockler, N. and Reardon, M. (eds.) *The BERA-SAGE international handbook of research-informed education policy and practice*. London: SAGE.

Daley, M., Orr, K. and Petrie, J. (2015) *Further education and the twelve dancing princesses*. London: IoE Press.

Elliott, G. (1996) 'Why is research invisible in further education?', *British Educational Research Journal*, 22(1), pp. 101–111.

Lloyd, C. and Jones, S. (2018) 'Researching the sector from within: the experience of establishing a research group within an FE college', *Research in Post-Compulsory Education*, 23(1), pp. 75–93. doi: 10.1080/13596748.2018.1420731

Pring, R. (2007) *John Dewey: a philosopher of education for our time?* New York: Continuum.

Index

Note: Page numbers in *italic* indicate a figure; page numbers in **bold** indicate a table.

2011 Skills for Life Survey 34

Academic Development department 6
Academic Partners (APs) 106, 109
action research 2, 5, 6, 36, 43, 55, 59, 60, 77, 80–81, 83, 84, 86, 91–100, 103, 111, 112, 114, 116, 143
adult community and family learning (ACL) 77–78, 80
adult literacy 31–35
age 43, 114, 134, 135
agency 9, 13, 16, 22, 35, 81, 96, 141, 142, 144
Agriculture Act, 2020 52
agriculture in Further Education 49–55
aims/objectives of research 32, 38–39, 77, 102, 111–112, 130
Armstrong, E.G. 61, 63
Arnold, R. 4, 97, 142, 143, 147
Association for Research in Post-Compulsory Education (ARPCE) 12, 13
Association of Colleges Senior Leadership Development Programme 131
Atkins, L. 120
authentic leadership 131, 135
autonomy 7, 8, 13, 99, 112, 117
Avis, J. 142

Ball, S. J. 105
barriers to research xx, 2, 5–7, 32
barriers to engagement with CPD 118–121
Barton, D. 33
Bedford College Group Research Network 8, 10–11

Beighton, C. 22
Bernstein, B. 13
biographical-narrative-interpretive model 133
Bound, H. 120
Bourke, B. 103
Bowyer, J. 69

Cahill, J. 69
cameras on/cameras off (Roberts) 99–100
capacity: of research 1–2, 15–16, 94, 102–103, 109, 118–125, 144, 147; development of, 107, 124, 143–144
Chen, J. 119, 144
coding 43, 53, 63–64
collaboration 9, 14, 21, 49, 83, 84, 92, 97, 104, 115, 137, 141
Collaborative Research in Practice (report) 9
College Action Inquiry Research Network (CAIRN) 108
college-based higher education (CBHE) 67–75; *see also* course leaders (CLs) for college-based higher education
College Development Network (CDN) 107–108
College Group 68, 72; Chief Executive of 69–70; staff structure in 69, *70*
community learning 2, 6, 77, 80, 147
community of practice 13–14, 33, 86, 99, 112, 145
consultation 137
Continuous Professional Development (CPD) 11, 21, 118, 143; existing market for 120–124; improvement in

attendance 59–65; improvement in provision of 118; knowledge, usage of 119–120; management support for 11
Contract of Employment 71, 72
Convenors' Group 10
course leaders (CLs) for college-based higher education: Contract of Employment 71, 72; defined 69; employment contracts 68; everyday work of 67; interviews with 67–74; methodology, 69–70, timetables 71–72; working of 69
Covid-19 pandemic 10, 16, 123, 132
creation of roles for research with FE 144–145
Culture of Curiosity 92; college-wide strategic objective 93; college-wide vision 93; examples of 99–100; findings and conclusions 97–99; framework for *98*; teaching and learning vision 94
Curriculum Manager in a Further/Higher Education College in Northern Ireland 6

data: collection and analysis 5, 16, 74, 114, 133, *133–134*; saturation 53; types and sources 69–70, **70**
Degener, S. 34
Derrick, J. 119
Department for Education 16, 33, 118, 123
desk-based research approach 108–109
democracy 2, 13, 14, 112, 145
diffraction/diffractive analysis 23, *23*, 25
digital self-evaluation 91
discourse 29, 74, 105, 107
dissemination 11, 15, 124
diversity of research in sector 8
diversity of the FE sector 1, 2, 105, 120
doctoral studies 2, 4, 24, 146
doings, practice architectures 14
Drake, P. 130
Duncan, S. 119
Dweck, C. S. 40
dysfunction 136–137

early career (EC) framework 16–17, 137
East London Advanced Technology Training (ELATT) 80

East Midlands Centre for Excellence in Teacher Training (emCETT) 77
educational background 5, 7, 135–136
Education and Training Foundation (ETF) 5, 8, 13–16, 77, 80, 81, 131; Practitioner Research Programme 15
Education Endowment Foundation (EEF) 78
effective leadership 7, 137
Elliott, G. 12, 104
'Emojis in ESOL and English' 80
empathy gap 4, 38, 39, 41–42, 45, 142
employment contract 68, 71, 72, 74; *see also* Contract of Employment
empower/empowerment 6, 8, 14, 16, 47, 63, 84, 86, 92, 93, 97, 100, 114, 137, 145
engagement of management teams with research 15, 40, 94–95, 99, 111, 145
engagement, of students 39–41
environmental changes, impact of 49, 51
ESOL (English for Speakers of Other Languages) 77; existing context 80; usage of knowledge in 78–80
ethics 16, 69, 114, 120, 122
evaluative model of observation 21, 22, 24
everyday writing 4, 32, 34–36

face-to-face training 63
failure mindset 38–43, 45, 47; *see also* mindset
Feed the tree 95–97
feedback 4, 5, 21, 25, 26, 45, 62, 77, 78, 81, 95, 96, 114, 137
FEResearchmeet 2, 8, 12–14, 16, 145
festival of practice 96, 97, 99
food poverty 95
framework for peer observation 25, **27–29**
functionally literate 33
functional skills 33
funding 9, 11, 42, 60, 107, 118, 119, 124
Further Education and Skills (FES) 14
Further Education Development Agency (FEDA) 9
Further Education Research Association (FERA) 12
Further and Higher Education college 111

Gallagher, C. 24
GCSE Resit project 4, 17, 38–41, 47, 118–119, 121, 123, 142
gender 25, 134
glass ceiling 134, 137
Good Friday Agreement 113
'good' teaching, as defined by Ofsted 24
'good' teaching' development of 24
Gosling, D. 24
grammatical analysis 32, 35
Great FE Teaching: Sharing Good Practice 8
Grief workshops 62–63
growth of interest in research xvii, 103
growth mindset 40; *see also* mindset
Guba, E.G. 52

Hamilton, M. 33
Hammond, A. 69
Hayward, G. 119
healthcare professionals, reducing barriers to improve attendance 59–64; present scenario 59–60
Heath, L. 130
Higher Education Funding Council for England (HEFCE) 73
Hordern, J. 119, 120
hourly paid lecturers 136
Huggett, A. 97
Hynes, C. 141–142

identity 4, 10, 31, 35, 52, 102, 104, 108, 112, 129–132, 134, 135, 141, 142, 146
incorporation 117, 131
Individual Learning Plans (ILPs) 78–79
Initial Teacher Education (ITE) 21
institutional ethnography 67, 69
intergenerational learning spaces *see* project-based learning (PBL)
interpretivism 50, 62
interventions 4, 38, 39, 42, 43, 45, 47, 62, 83, 107, 121
interviews 50, 121, **122**; coding 53; with course leaders 67–74; life history 133, *133–134*; questions 51–53, *122*; semi-structured 52–53; transcription of 53
Ivanič, R. 33

Jacobson, E. 34
James, D. 105
Jones, S. 2, 7, 10, 94, 119, 142, 143
Jupp, T. 131

Kelchtermans, G. 51, 55
Kind, V. 51
Kline, N. 115
knowledge, usage of 22–24; agriculture in Further Education 50–51; continuous professional development 119–120; ESOL (English for Speakers of Other Languages) 78–80; project-based learning 113–114; *Skills for Life* project 33–34; Teach the Teacher intervention 40–41
Korek, S. 69

land-based education 49–50, 52, 55
language 2, 33–34, 78–79, 83–85, 94, 120, 122
Lasky, A. 95
leadership of research 2, 61, 63, 91–93, 105, 111, 129–132, 141, 145–146
leaders/leadership, researching stories of: education 135–136; authentic 131, 135; effective 7, 137; existing context 132; family background 135; FE 129–137; life history interviews 133, *133–134*; and management 131–132; opportunities for 136; professional identity 132; research findings 134–137; work 136
learner engagement 39, 40–41, 81, 83, 93–95, 111
learning: community 2, 6, 77, 80; diary 81, 83, *84–85*, 85,
lifelong 92, 97; movement of 31–36; probation 31–32, 34–35; professional 6, 91–92, 95, 98, 103; project-based learning 113–114; teaching and 92, 94
Learning and Skills Research Network (LSRN) 8, 9–10, 16, 17n3
Learning and Teaching Academy (LTA) 107
Learning and Work Institute (LWI) 78
learning diaries: initial reflection page from *84*; learner ownership of 85; online 85; research findings related to 81–83, *82*; session reflection page from *85*

lesson reflection pages *82*
life experiences 7, 130–132, 135
lifelong learning 92, 97
limitations of studies 5, 55, 143
Lincoln, Y.S. 52
literacy 31–36, 81
literature reviews 5, 61–62, 63, 121; agriculture 51; CPD 118–119; observation 55
Lloyd, C. 10, 141
'locked out' by language 120
Lundberg, M. 132

Making Learning Happen (Race) 78
managerial support/buy-in 59, 61, 63, 67, 104, 105, 119, 141
mapping: barriers 103–105; defined 69; ideas for 116; of interference 23; sector 8–17
Martin-Chang, S. 114
Maslin-Prothero, S.E. 61
masters studies 2, 4, *42, 44, 46, 47*, 106, 111, 136, 146
McCann, J. 104
McClintock, B. 114
McMahon, G.T. 61
McNiff, J. 80
methodologies: agriculture in Further Education 52; community learning 80–81; CBHE 69–70; Culture of Curiosity 95–97; development of new 15, 17, 119, 143–144; FE leadership 132–133; healthcare professionals 62; intergenerational learning spaces 114; modelled 124; new 15, 119; offender learning 35; RCG 7; Scottish colleges 108–109; teaching and learning 92; teaching practice development 25; Teach the Teacher (TTT) intervention 43, *44*; theorise and development 146
mindset 40; concepts of 42; failure 4, 38, 43, 45; FEC 102; fixed 40; students 115; theory 40; VESPA 15; *see also* growth mindset
misunderstandings of learner 51, 53
mobilization, of skills between contexts 34
movement of learning 31–36

National Education Union (NEU) 13
National Health Service (NHS) 5, 59, 62, 65

Naz, Z. 22
New Public Management (NPM) 68, 73, 74; *see also* performativity
non-attendance at CPD, reasons for 61–63
non-attendance at CPD having impact on skills 60
Northern Ireland 2, 6, 113

observation 22; as methodological tool 24; peer 25, **27–29**
observations of teaching and learning (OTL) 21, 22
Offenders' Learning and Skills Service (OLASS) 31
Ofsted 11, 22, 24
O'Leary, M. 22
Online art exhibition (Sedgwick) 100
online learning diary 85
Outstanding Teaching, Learning and Assessment (OTLA) 13, 14–15, 79–80
ownership 1, 24, 80, 83, 85, 96, 111, 114, 119–120

parity of esteem 3, 94, 95, 118, 119, 121, 124, 146
participant checking 50, 52–55
Pathways of Excellence 91; self-evaluation process and 92; *see also* Culture of Curiosity
pedagogical awareness 4, 26, 49–51, 53, 54
pedagogical choices 25–26
pedagogical content knowledge (PCK) 51
pedagogical conversations 21, 25–26, 147
pedagogy 2, 4–5, 24, 32, 35–36, 50, 141
peer observation, framework for 25, **27–29**
peer sharing 21
performativity 13, 22–23, 105, 107–109, 141
Pesco, D. 114
pick and mix style pages, learning diary 84
PLR (Personal Learning Record) 77, 78
policy changes, impact of 51–52, 99, 143

Index

positionality 32, 39–40, 112–113, 130–131; agriculture in Further Education 50; CBHE 67–68; community learning 77–78; Culture of Curiosity 94–95; FE leadership 130–131; healthcare professionals 59–60; intergenerational learning spaces 112–113; offender learning 32; Research College Group (RCG) 119; Scottish colleges 102–103; teaching practice development 22; Teach the Teacher (TTT) intervention 39–40
positive relationships 7, 15, 39, 45
post-compulsory education (PCE) 8, 12, 22, 94
post-doctoral work 2, 4, 24, 49, 146
Post Graduate Certificate in Education (PGCE) 59, 60
power 25, 41, 81, 111, 114, 117, 145
practice development 6, 9, 14, 22, 36, 51, 60, 107, 119, 124–125
practice knowledge, use of 1, 13–14, 33–34, 36, 50–51, 81, 119–120, 142
Practitioner Led Action Research (PLAR) programme 77, 83
Practitioner Research Projects (PRPs) 14, 15
Pring, R. 142
probation learning 31–32, 34–35
professional context 129
professional identity 129–132, 135, 137, 141–142
professionalism 1, 129, 141, 147
professional learning 6, 91–92, 95, 98, 103
project-based learning (PBL): knowledge, usage of 113–114; research findings 115–116
protected time 63–64
pseudonyms 52, 133
Purcell-Gates, V. 34

quality framework 72
questioning **27–28**
questions *see* interview questions; research questions

race 134–135
Race, P. 78

Ramani, S. 61
RARPA (Recognising and Recording Progress and Achievement) 77, 78–79, *79*
recognition and crediting of those undertaking research work 145
reflection/reflective practice 22–23, *23*, 31, 62, 77–78, 81, *82*, 83, *84–85*
relatings, practice architectures 14
Rendell, C. 69
renumeration of research work 124
research: existing context 51–52; findings 53–54; journey 6, 8, 38, 41, 65, 83, 98, 111, 116–117; methodology used in 52–53; research questions 49–50
research, making meaning 62, 80–81, 208
Research and Enhancement Centre (College Development Network) 108, 109
Research College Group (RCG) 2–3, 16–17, 118–124
research culture, development of 2, 11, 15, 91–92, 96–98, 103–106, 142, 144–145
researcher: bias 39, 61–62, 103, 113; leaving the sector 144; positionality 50
Research Further scheme 9
Research in Post-Compulsory Education (RPCE) 12
research questions 21, 60–61, 121; aims and objectives 32, 38–39, 77, 102, 111–112, 130; agriculture in Further Education (FE) 49–50; community learning 77; CBHE 67; Culture of Curiosity 92–94; FE leadership 130; healthcare professionals 60–61; intergenerational learning spaces 111–112; offender learning 32; Research College Group (RCG) 118–119; Scottish colleges 102; *Skills for Life* project 32; teaching practice development 21; Teach the Teacher intervention 38–39;
research questions/aims and objectives 32, 38–39, 77, 102, 111–112, 130
resilience 10, 40–42, 60, 64
resit policy 39, 42–43

restraints on sector 144
restructures 136
right to withdraw, participants 133
Roberts, C. 99–100
role modelling 116, 131, 143–144
role reversal 38–39, 45, 47, 97
Rowley, J. 103

Sandwell College 11
sayings, practice architectures 14
Scattergood, K. 36
Scottish further education colleges: initiatives for fostering research and scholarly activities within 106; structural and cultural barriers 103–105
Sedgwick, K. 100
Self Assessment Report (SAR) 77
self-evaluation: competencies 91–92; digital 91
semi-structured interviews 52–53
senior leaders 7, 93, 95–96, 99, 129–137
Shulman, L.S. 51
sickness 60, 63
Skills for Life project 31; class of learners 34–35; findings 35–36; knowledge, usage of 33–34
SMART targets 79, 83
Smith, D.E 34, 69
Smith, G. 61
Smith, L. 119
Smith, R. 24
social class 135
social inclusion/justice 32, 81, 105, 108, 112
Society for Education and Training (SET) 13, 100
Soler, M. 34
Solihull College & University Centre 7, 94
Solvason, C. 104
space 1, 10–13, 38, 71, 99–100, 102–103, 111–117, 120–121, 144–147
staff shortages 60
status of sector 94, 106, 119, 124
Steering Committee, Research College Group 16–17, 118–124
Stenhouse, L. 31, 80
stories 4, 7, 22, 36, 113, 129–130
strategy, alignment to 84, 106

students, emotional wellbeing: autonomy 7, 99, 112, 117; barriers for 60–61, 103–104; connection to local environment 7; engagement with activities 4; impact of pedagogical risk taking on 22; mindset 4, 40, 115; relationship to teacher 40–42, 45; as researchers 51–55, 107, 111–116; thinking time for 26; understanding of teacher materials 51; working class 113

tacit knowledge 51
target setting 78
Taylerson, Lynne 14
Teacher Education 120
Teacher Education research 22–23, 120
teacher-researcher 31
teacher-student relationships (TSRs) 41–42
Teach the Teacher (TTT) intervention 38, 97, 147; findings of 43, 45, *46*; knowledge, usage of 40–41; learner engagement 41; methodology 97; resit policy 42–43; teacher-student relationships 41–42
ThingLink 122, *123*
Thinking Rounds (Kline) 115
timetables, course leaders 71–72
time to research 5, 32, 67–69, 78, 92–93, 102–104, 106, 119–121, 133, 144
transformation 42
'Transformative Teaching and Learning in Further Education' (University and College Union) 112
Tresham College 11
trust 39, 83, 91, 97, 131
trustworthiness, features of 52
Tummons, J. 120

undergraduate research 31
University and College Union (UCU) 112
University of the Highlands and Islands (UHI) 103, 106–107, 109
utility of work 1, 119, 147

values: personal 80, 86, 144; of researchers 9, 119
VESPA mindset programme 15
video, use in observations 25–27

visibility of research in the Further Education (FE) 8
vocational education 50, 111
vocational pedagogy 10, 50
voice 1, 13, 69, 95–97, 115–116, 119–120, 141, 147

warrant 142–143, 146
Wengraf, T. 133

what works 16, 50–51
'Why Research is Still Invisible in Further Education' (Solvason and Elliott) 104
workload 5, 61, 64, 68, 71–74, 92, 113, 119, 144
writing framework 2–3

Young, P. 104

For Product Safety Concerns and Information please contact our EU representative GPSR@taylorandfrancis.com
Taylor & Francis Verlag GmbH, Kaufingerstraße 24, 80331 München, Germany

www.ingramcontent.com/pod-product-compliance
Lightning Source LLC
Chambersburg PA
CBHW070309230426
43664CB00015B/2695